Biographia
Floridiana

Biographia Floridiana

Essaying Florida

To essay: "to attempt to explain"

Lamar York

www.biographiafloridiana.com

Editors: Bradford Taylor, Chase Robinson, Lee Horsman
Cover design: Bradford Taylor
Back cover photo: Lee Horsman

Pine Level Press
Oxford • Burnsville

ISBN:
ISBN-13: 978-1725719750

To Florida…For Florida…

CONTENTS

ACKNOWLEDGEMENTS

Grateful acknowledgement to:

The Florida Historical Quarterly
The Marjorie Kinnan Rawlings Journal of Florida Literature
Tampa Review
Southern Studies: An Interdisciplinary Journal of the South

where some of these essays first appeared.

Special thanks to family and to Bradford Taylor,
who made this book happen.

PREFACE

In September 1953, a young new teacher, Miss Eleanor Langlois, walked into my tenth grade English classroom at Wildwood High School and wrote on the blackboard "essai-essay: to essay is to attempt to explain." She began to talk about the essay as a literary form: take a point of view about something of little consequence and make it interesting by the language employed to write about that topic. She went on to describe the work of essayists Charles Lamb, William Hazlitt, Thomas De Quincey, Michel de Montaigne, Francis Bacon and, as became clear, her favorite, Robert Louis Stevenson. I have thought of her since as my Essayist-in-Chief.

Miss Langlois was gone after one year, back to graduate school. But by the end of that sophomore year I had an entirely new appreciation for the English essay. I was sure this was the genre for me, though I didn't yet know about literary genres. As a result of her class, I was committed to the essay. I never dreamed I might write a poem, or a play, certainly not a whole novel, but here was a form, which I had known heretofore only as a class assignment, and it seemed possible to actually learn to write an essay with the model in mind that we now had explained to us and had practiced. I was eager for my next assignment.

Before that sophomore year was over, we read Shakespeare, George Eliot, Nathaniel Hawthorne and others. A great discovery for me was Samuel Taylor Coleridge. I had heard of "The Rime of the Ancient Mariner," but was totally unprepared for "Kubla Khan" and the description of Xanadu. The greatest treasure for me lay in the pages of Coleridge's autobiography, *Biographia Literaria*. I could not get far in the prose of the text; it was not light reading for a high school sophomore. But it was not the text that would hold my attention so much as it was the astonishing title, *Biographia Literaria*. This title became my talisman, and I've thought often of someday using the title—for something really important.

Moving from Wildwood High School to Florida State University, the essay became much more serious. Essaying about the whole range of English prose and poetry from Beowulf to William Faulkner nearly convinced me that essaying meant literary criticism exclusively, at least for me, as Coleridge had meant the essay. FSU meant the bare minimum of science, but otherwise all things English. My campus haunts were Strozier Library, the Presbyterian Center English Coffee Hour on Friday, Conradi Theater, the Leon County library in The Columns, Professors Ben Carroll, Sarah Goodman, Griffith Pugh, Carmen Rogers, George Yost, Claude Flory and others. FSU and Tallahassee meant Westcott Hall, LeRoy Collins, Goodwood, Wakulla Springs, the old Capitol, and driving Agriculture Commissioner Nathan Mayo, which meant all things Florida.

Then, after five years learning to teach, it was on to Atlanta, and a very different life, but never far in mind from Florida. Atlanta meant the Atlanta Symphony and Ballet, Emory Village, Piedmont Park, raising my kids with the help of Fernbank Elementary and Druid Hills High, but most of all it meant DeKalb College, where I found my vocation. I thought I had learned to teach at North Florida Junior College, but after rural Madison, Florida, the international cast of characters at DeKalb meant African, Asian, Latin American, Fijian, Iranian and more; an astonishing mix of students and colleagues from everywhere with whom I could talk about essays.

But most of all, it meant the launching and editing of the campus literary magazine, *The Chattahoochee Review*, which came into being in 1981. This put me in touch with writers everywhere. Now I moved from teaching freshman English essay writing to editing the writing of professional writers from around the world. This was a different way altogether of working with the essay.

Soon, I would envy those writers so much that I would get back to my own essaying and to writing about Florida, where everything was grist for the essay mill. Unforgettable childhood hours in my grandfather's barn and hayloft and slaughterhouse, to more exotic Florida scenes such as Tampa's Ybor City, the Fuller Warren Bridge over the St. Johns River, the Seaboard Railroad where my father worked, the Castillo de San Marcos, the Wahoo Swamp, Osceola, the Green Swamp, Panasoffkee, Dade Park, Okahumpka, Mars Hill Primitive Baptist Church, Cedar Key, the Withlacoochee River, heroes like Cabeza de Vaca and Osceola, and Oxford, to such ordinary delights as guavas and smoked mullet.

With the Southerner's love of homeplace, and Southern writing's concentration on sense of place, writing about Florida naturally appealed to me as the subject in which I could express my own voice and as the subject of the biography I would write. These essays have become my larger "biographia"; not a biographia literaria, but my *Biographia Floridiana*.

INTRODUCTION

A Floridian, Dr. John Gorrie, invented an ice-making machine in Apalachicola in 1851. He fanned air down over his ice and on to patients to cool fevered brows. Gorrie's ice machine and air-cooling apparatus was regarded as medical equipment until air-conditioning was invented in 1902, installed in a home in 1914, and into a car in 1939. Without it Florida might well be the thirty-sixth most populous state in the union, as it was in 1900, and not today's third largest. Yet Florida feels mostly busy, not third in everything among the states. It feels as if it were important only historically, until tourists became populous.

The heart of the eastern US, from the Gulf to Canada, bears a primordial Florida name. Yet despite its long history, Florida does not yet play as sophisticated a role in national affairs as the state it recently replaced as third largest. Florida's civil dynamic is transiency. It has five times the number of tourists as residents, and state policy often favors the transient. Numbers of home-owning, registered voters in Florida enjoy mild winters and the absence of income taxes, but also live elsewhere. The state pays its bills with a regressive tax. It spends inordinately on incarceration, meagerly on conservation. Once, leaders expanded a century-old system of two universities into a network of eleven. Later leaders imploded higher education to expand incarceration. Recent leaders implemented steps to enable top-tier campuses to achieve national prominence. Still, Mickey summons multitudes to an illusory magic; the common good would better be served by a summons from the unconquerable Seminole.

The dynamic of Florida's natural life involves delicate flora and fauna, rivers and springs, not indestructible rock mountains, vast deserts, deep canyons, or endless treeless prairies. Florida's glory is water and wind, beach and swamp, rapidly being lost to population and pollution. In Florida's poisoned political climate, "global warming" and "climate change" are censored language. Though Florida has a world-class national park of endless savannas, it is the most fragile of all the great national parks.

Some musings in these essays may seem more wistful than prophetic, given they were written before the impact of climate change on the state became so startlingly clear. Though humans made much of the magic of Florida, the more vital, primal part of that magic is the work of nature. None of it is permanent or immutable, as deserts or rock mountains often seem to be. Scientists say that by 2100, Florida may change shape more than any other state in the nation, possibly losing long stretches of coast to the sea. Perhaps Florida's great contribution to the future could be raising awareness about our changing planet.

How does Florida continue to mesmerize? These essays attempt to illustrate the guileless charm of one of the world's first choices among the perfect places to be, a choice shared by the author.

1

Essaying Florida: "From the Perdido..."

I'm retiring and moving to Florida. That I am not pulling up stakes in a place like Detroit or Chicago is all that ameliorates the crass familiarity of this next move. I'm just one state removed now. Still, I feel silly, almost, telling friends I'm retiring and moving to Florida. "Of course," they say, "you and everybody else your age. So, what else is new?" But, I want to insist, I am not guilty of the great American hegira to warmer climes, particularly Florida. Of all the nomadic paradigms of Americans—white flight to suburbia, crisscrossing the country at the behest of corporate headquarters--the one I least expected ever to imitate is to retire from a working life spent elsewhere and move to Florida. So I think of this next move not as retiring but as returning to Florida. I've got family there, and roots.

I lived in Florida my first thirty years. Now I've lived in Georgia thirty years. I don't have another thirty years left, but whatever is left will be spent in Florida, it appears. I've lived my life in the capitals of the two states, Tallahassee and Atlanta. The place I'm retiring to was the terminus of the first railroad in Florida. Atlanta, where I've lived in Georgia, was called Terminus, because the first railroad stopped there. Yet close together as they are, Georgia and Florida are also very different places. And in them, I've been very different persons.

Life in the two states offer counterpoint—Florida palms, Georgia pines. It's not just that I am a thousand feet higher in the air in Georgia than in Florida. It isn't just that in Florida I was a country boy, while in Georgia I've been a city man. In Florida, I was always a young man, just as Ponce de León had promised, full of the hardihood of youth, unable to imagine how high I might ultimately rise in the world, but ambitiously sure it would be high. In Georgia, I've always been older, maturer, more like Georgia's serious, colony-building chief executive James Oglethorpe than the romantic wanderer de León. In Georgia, I've pretty much known exactly how far I might go, known that the highest I'd go in Georgia was the highest I'd get in life. In Florida, I was a little fish in a small pond. My hometown, my high school, even then my university, seemed small potatoes. Though Florida has come to be regarded lately as a notable place to be from, I think of it as I knew it then, and even life in the capital was small town. In Georgia, it's been little fish in a big pond for me all the way. Atlanta wasn't as highrise then as it is now, but even when I first arrived there Atlanta thought of itself as an important place to be. Maybe that's why a sleepy fishing village on the almost never ruffled shores of the Big Bend Gulf Coast of Florida seems so appealing.

As I begin to think and plan toward the reverse migration, I wonder what kind of Florida awaits me. When I left, it had five million people and was just beginning to think of itself among the really big states of the union. Neil Armstrong had shot off from Cape Canaveral to the moon, but the Mariel-to-Miami boatlift had not commenced, a later journey that would affect Florida's destiny far beyond what a walk on the moon has, reminiscent more of history than of future, of a time when all of man's most immemorial journeys were made over calm or stormy seas, not via the air. Though now securely beyond the original motivation for the space race, the life-and-death struggle with Russia, a race which once had Florida's leaders licking their chops over just how much federal largess might eventually end up in the state, the population nevertheless continues to explode, relentlessly overturning wilderness.

The electorate in Florida has turned decidedly away from itself as a place of second chances to the less forgiving, inflexible new national model. All that benevolent sunshine might just naturally have been expected to foster a more tolerant, inclusive spirit of commonweal. And it will again, in a future day. Florida is, after all, a naturally happy, casual sort of place. But first it must become more comfortable with its new position among the leading states. Florida's distinction will necessarily have to be invented along lines unlike those already patented by earlier greats. Yet one feels perceptible movement in that direction, moves that sometime reveal how much ground is yet to be gained. When I left Florida thirty years ago, no Florida college football team had even come close to winning the national championship. Interstate 75 was almost complete from Naples to Chicago. My mother and father, the sixth generation of us to come to life in Sumter County, were both still alive and still at home, where home had always been. The Methodist church I left behind was still unflinchingly segregated.

Now I go back, to natal origins I wonder if I will recognize, if scenes I once never expected to leave will offer even the slightest familiarity. My old high school, built by my grandfather as chairman of the Sumter County school board, and attended by both of my parents, as well as all the rest of their generation and mine, was torn down years ago, a new modern one-story air-conditioned textile factory look-alike erected on the outskirts of town. New schools are required to insure the necessary parking space for each and every student, all of whom drive to school these days, even if home is just across the street. In Tallahassee, the state capitol, a 1902 structure where I once had a basement office as chauffeur to the Commissioner of Agriculture for the State of Florida, is now a museum, towered over by a high-rise shaft of an insurance headquarters-style office building. The FSU that I attended had 7,000 students, all campus residents. Today it has 35,000 students, is always hungry for more, and has awarded more PhDs than it once had undergraduates. It was a girls-only college until ten years before I matriculated. Now it has national championships in football.

So sure that the Florida I knew won't feel like home, I begin to reconstruct my own idea of Florida, one that I can return to at least in memory, knowing the new place called Florida to have become a most remarkably newly made place. Unsure of how I will feel about contemporary Florida, and knowing myself incapable of relocating the place I left, I begin to reproduce a Florida based on the only design I have any control over, that is, the one in my head. Florida has always exercised my imagination, so much so that I decorated my boyhood bedroom with a flag of Florida rather than the one of choice of most boyhood friends, the ubiquitous Confederate battle flag.

In a serious young manhood my love of Florida expanded beyond the state flag. I began collecting books and maps about Florida. In time, this collection acquired the dimensions of a respectably antiquarian shelf of early histories and travel guides. Florida has somehow always appealed to the imagination of the bookish traveler; because Florida cities feel so new, the many travel guides to early Florida seem as exotic now as the Florida wilderness must have seemed to those long-ago writer-travelers. I came to own a bookcase groaning with Florida materials by the time I knew I would return there, the passion of Florida never having abandoned me. Now, in a remarkably self-satisfying moment, I would sit down in my own library and literally recreate a Florida of my choosing. There were enough pictures and drawings, Seminole vocabularies, histories and descriptions to allow me a substantial canvas on which to draw the earliest of Floridas. This one I could do in my own library. I could recreate Florida just like I wanted to think of it, even before I packed up my books and left Georgia.

In an odd moment of clarity, I chose not the oldest book there on my shelves, momentarily denying my antiquarian inclinations, but rather the one that seemed the most authoritative, the very Constitution of the state I had left thirty years earlier and now proposed returning to. But the initial effort to recreate Florida from the ground up would offer a big surprise. The first definers of Florida began in what seemed like the least likely place for a beginning of Florida. For any traveler since the beginning of map making or regularly scheduled ship travel to the New World, the choice of beginnings for a description of Florida would naturally be an Atlantic Coast landing in a straight trajectory from a point of European embarkation. So the writers of Florida's official constitution in 1845 seemed strained to find the natural starting point. In fact, what they had written there a century and a half ago sounded wildly off base: "Commencing at the mouth of the River Perdido hence north to Alabama...." The River Perdido? Doesn't Perdido mean "lost?" Doesn't that name of that river suggest that those original constitutional definers didn't know where to start Florida? They started at the intersection with Alabama. But isn't that the tail, rather than the head, of Florida? Wouldn't anyone thinking about Florida just naturally, instinctively begin at its southernmost place? Or wouldn't it start at the historical beginning, St. Augustine? Is it possible for Florida to begin anywhere else? Perhaps at Key West, or perhaps at the mouth of the great north-flowing St. Johns. But the Perdido? The framers of the legal entity of Florida took as their beginning the most northwesterly spot possible and still be in Florida. Can anyone imagine the New World from any other than an Atlantic Coast first-sighting? Surely anyone familiar with the map of Florida—and isn't everyone?—would start somewhere else.

Surely, virtually anyone familiar with the bird-eye's view of Florida, famous long before satellites made such a picture possible to people as well as to birds, would begin at the most southerly point of the state. And if not there, then, perhaps at the northeastern corner, the St. Marys River, dividing the state from Georgia and the rest of the United States, as it was for so long in history. The very proximity of any point on the east coast of Florida to the same Atlantic that brought almost everyone else here, from Ponce de León on, would seem to dictate a modern description commencing somewhere on the Atlantic, not the most northwesterly point of the Gulf Coast of Florida. And then to proceed "hence to Alabama"? For centuries, Florida had more in common with Havana than with Alabama, a mean three hundred years nearly to the date after Ponce de León came here directly from Cuba, initiating a Spanish run—Havana to St. Augustine—that endured until Andrew Jackson redefined territorial acquisition as the guiding principal of American expansionism.

However much history seems weighted in any other direction, though, starting at the most northwesterly point is exactly how the originators imagined what has become of one of the world's most recognizable political shapes, the corporate entity Florida. Leonardo da Vinci sat in his study in Florence beneath a map that showed the appellation "Florida" applied to everything in the New World. Leonardo could see a new world, stretching "from the great cape of Juan Ponce de León" northward to Labrador, all of it called "the continent called Florida." If Spanish, rather than English, had obtained as the language of the ultimate conquerors, North America would today be known as Florida. But the drawers of the corporate entity did not belong to an era characterized by the imagination of the likes of Columbus, or Ponce de León, or Leonardo. The men of the nineteenth century, alas, were not working with ideas or heroics but with the more basic possibilities of capitalism and nationalism, both of which seemed in almost limitless abundance in earliest Florida.

Maybe the constitutional definers began in Pensacola because the Florida they confronted existed then in only two places, and they had to choose one or the other. Florida consisted of only two cities, Pensacola and St. Augustine, four hundred miles apart. Nothing recognizably Florida lay in the four hundred fifty miles south of St. Augustine until one arrived at the very end, Key West. If anything existed between, it was known at best by loose renderings of Calusa or Tequesta names and was thus deemed inappropriate to English language maps and descriptions of the proud new corporate entity. Richard Fitzpatrick, South Florida's single representative to the constitutional convention that decided to commence at the Perdido, spoke for all thirty thousand square miles from the Hillsborough River east to the Indian River south to Mallory Docks, an area that today is seventeen counties and ten million people. One wonders how he felt about drawing up the outlines of the state from a Pensacola beginning rather than a Key West starting point. Nevertheless, draw it they did, in constitutional convention at St. Joseph, halfway between Pensacola and St. Augustine. St. Joseph would disappear in a pestilence, but the work done there to define Florida was, even with its Alpha and Omega at Perdido, sufficient to the day. According to Florida's first modern historian, George R. Fairbanks, writing in *Florida: It's History and Romance* in 1898, "It was by all odds the ablest body of men ever assembled in Florida," before or since, he might conclude today, and "the constitution then formed...is in many respects superior to the emendations since made."

And so Florida, old in Spanish but as yet young in English, wobbly as a new-born colt, became a political unit ostensibly equal to those states where English had long predominated. Florida entered into union with them on March 3, 1845, with 54,477 inhabitants. Delegates to the constitutional convention sensibly set the governor's salary at a modest $1,500, the secretary of state's at $600, members of the legislature at $3 daily plus mileage on horseback. The real estate value of the entire state was easily exceeded in value by the value of all the slaves in the state. Together, these came to a grand aggregate of eighty million dollars. The most pressing problem was whether the electorate would go for the argument to make two states of Florida, East and West, both open to slavery, which would have ended the balance of power in the U.S. Senate between free and slave states.

Florida is east and west, but not in the way the original framers at St. Joseph meant. They perhaps were motivated to start drawing political Florida in the west because West Florida seemed more English than Spanish. East Florida, centered on St. Augustine, has since time immemorial been, despite intermittent control by the English, a Spanish domain. Beginning in the west continued the tradition throughout most of North America of giving preference to things English.

But the division east and west, Spanish versus English, would not long be the essential division of Florida. Florida is also north and south, rural and urban, just like most political entities, but the ultimate definition, even more easily observable than panhandle versus peninsula, is Gulf versus Atlantic littorals. One imagines starting to define Florida with the Atlantic side, but if for some reason one begins on the Gulf side, one still does not easily imagine Pensacola as the starting point at one certain spot. In Key West, these two points, the Atlantic and the Gulf, are one and the same. Having deliberately bypassed such an obvious starting place, the real reason for the decision of the original definers of Florida has to have been a desire to write up a continuum, a whole, unbroken line, like successfully peeling an orange in one long unbroken peel. So, from the mouth of the Perdido, up to Alabama, across to the Atlantic, down to Tortugas, and back up again to the mouth of the Perdido, was their only choice, so as to end at the place of the beginning, as the framers so plaintively wrote it. Thus do I write now, too, as I return to my own place of beginning.

When I am once again resident in Florida, I will draw it to my own satisfaction. The starting point for all my imaginary meanderings in whatever direction will be the tiny island called Cedar Key, some fifty miles west of where I had my earlier beginning in Florida. I choose Cedar Key not because Lt. Col. Robert E. Lee mailed his wife a letter from there on February 13, 1849, while on a commission from the U.S. army to survey the Florida coast. He commenced his survey, not incidentally, at the St. Marys in the northeast corner and then went south, then west, in a proper survey of the longest state coast of the lower forty-eight states. He noted in his report to Washington that Cedar Key shipped 2,234 bales of cotton, 2,000 bales of hides and skins the previous year. I choose Cedar Key not for its exports but because from here I look out at the diamonds on the mullet-broken surface of the placid Gulf and realize, more clearly than I have in any other place, that this is where I can sit and think about what is happening to Florida, and what happens to me now that I am back here. For years I went to the Georgia mountains north of Atlanta to do my thinking about anything really important, but something about the row after row of distant ridges always made me want to go see what was over the next smoky rise rather than sit still to find out what might be lurking in my own imagination. Here at the Gulf's edge, the traffic of fewer people than live in my Atlanta apartment building to distract, I know that I can concentrate on my own idea of Florida. The map on my wall will be the familiar, indeed, famous panhandle and peninsula, Gulf and Atlantic; my flag will be the long-established if carpetbag-designed red saltier of St. Andrew on a field of white, intersecting at the "Indian female scattering flowers"; my taxes will go to Tallahassee again, rather than to Atlanta. But however real those definitions, the Florida that takes shape once I am in Cedar Key to stay will be one made of memories, both mine and the writers of the Florida that exists today only in books. I will reconstruct a Florida now to suit myself.

The census whereby this Florida of my private imagination will know increase will not be the one taken in ten-year increments by the federal government. It will grow according to the number of volumes I find time to read. Not saving the cream for last, I will begin with the best, the Florida Marjories, and their best work—Rawlings's *Cross Creek* and Douglas's *Florida: The Long Frontier*. From these creators of a Florida of metaphor, I will go on to the early historians—John Lee Williams's *The Territory of Florida*, Bernard Roman's *A Concise Natural History of East and West Florida*—and more modern historians—Kenny, Proctor, Gannon, Jahoda, Tebeau. Florida has big problems, too big to be ignored, made understandable by such volumes as Williams Bradford Huie's *Ruby McCollum*, Anthony Powell's *Gideon's Trumpet*, James McMullen's *Cry of the Panther*, Mark Lane's *Arcadia*, John Rothchild's *Up For Grabs*, Alec Wilkinson's *Big Sugar*, and Michael

D'Orso's *Like Judgement Day*. Yet Florida is also still Eden, at least in the imagination, and that can easily be recreated in the inestimable work of the early naturalists. Henry Nehrling's *The Plant World in Florida*, Bradford Torrey Simpson's *Florida Wild Life*, Tom Barbour's *That Vanishing Eden*, Allen Andrew's *A Yank Pioneer in Florida*, John C. Gifford's studies, W.S. Blatchley's books, the work of Archie Carr and Jack Rudloe, Howell on birds: all tell the story of natural Florida. Florida's extraordinary natural beauty is so carefully explored in these volumes as to need no other defense in a rational world.

If such a shelf of books can't redeem Florida from its self, it may prove irredeemable. So I may turn to the tongue-in-cheek humor of early travel books, their Yankee concepts of allure reminding the reader that Florida has always been an object of more hyperbole than hard work to protect its fragile subtropical enticements. Those early Yankee travel books are legion, a library all by themselves: Clifton Johnson's *Highways and Byways of Florida*, Charles Hallock's *Camp Life in Florida*, James Henshall's *Camping and Cruising in Florida,* Charles Ledyard Norton's *A Handbook of Florida*, *Rambler's Guide to Florida*, George Barbour's *Florida for Tourists, Invalids, and Settlers*, Ledyard Bill's *A Winter in Florida,* W. Davidson's *Florida of Today, Silvia Sunshine's Petals Plucked from Sunny Climes,* F. R. Swift's *Florida Fancies*, Helen Harcourt's *Home Life in Florida*, Rhodes and Dumont's *A Guide to Florida*, but above all, the ever-complimentary Harriet Beecher Stowe's *Palmetto Leaves*.

More would seem superfluous by now, yet there is another whole library, one consisting of the belles-lettres of Florida. Like Southern literature in general, Florida claims more writers of fiction than poetry. Again the work of the Marjories provides a good beginning. *The Yearling* and *Road to the Sun* tell much of the story, yet there is an embarrassment of riches to come. Kirk Munroe, Edith Pope, Rubylea Hall, Mary Bethell Alfriend, Wyatt Blassingame, Zora Neale Hurston, Patrick Smith, Edwin Granberry, James Branch Cabell, Leon Griffith, Wesley Ford Davis, MacKinlay Kantor, Borden Deal, Andrew Lytle, Theodore Pratt, Harry Crews, Sterling Watson, Peter Matthiessen, Connie May Fowler, Carl Hiaasen, Charles Willeford, Shelley Fraser Mickle, and more round out a reading list that will create a Florida almost the rival of the original, the one first seen by Ponce de León among literate men.

I will not risk blurring my vision of the Florida of the imagination with interstates and high-rise beaches. One can find a real enough Florida in an excellent system of state parks. One can still go back to Cross Creek. It is enough for me that I was here to see an Orlando of pleasant neighborhoods nestled around small lakes. I remember when all the traffic on 301, the major thoroughfare right down through the heart of Florida, stopped at red lights that regulated traffic around the Marion County courthouse, right in the middle of Ocala, just as in any other small town down South. I remember Miccosukee Road leading northward out of Tallahassee, dark at noonday from interlaced oaks and mosses, the city skyline dominated by the oddly squared old silver dome. I remember Marineland as the premier attraction in the entire state, and far away the most expensive at $.75 per person over twelve. I remember Marco Island accessible only by boat, home to one old derelict fishing camp. I remember the old un-air-conditioned wooden jook at Salt Springs. In my own private Florida, a place that exists in metaphor and memory, it is all still there.

First published in *The Florida Historical Society Quarterly*, 82 (Winter 2004), 360-369.

2

Capital Images: Beach vs. Antiquity

History has become the natural ally of the tourist economy. Such popular vacation destinations as New Orleans, Santa Fe, or Charleston, would find it unthinkable to separate their history from their appeal. In Baltimore, old Fort McHenry is no more out of keeping with the popular waterfront than crabcakes and row housing. When Boston surfaces as a vacation destination, no advertising image need be made to connect the history surrounding Faneuil Hall or nearby Plymouth Rock with the cultural assets of modern Boston. In planning a vacation to Philadelphia, unlikely as that may seem, it takes no great leap of imagination to associate Independence Hall and the Liberty Bell with surrounding modern Philadelphia. That same natural connection seems to exist for the combination of vacation and cultural sites in more places than just established old cities. In a pastoral setting such as Virginia, for example, there is a natural connection between the history to be seen in Williamsburg, on one end of the state, and the natural beauty to be seen in the Shenandoah at the other end. But the same connection comes less readily to mind in the case of sites of America's oldest history near Florida's sandy beaches and theme parks. The image of Florida as, first, a beach vacation land and now a theme park vacation site, has been so pervasively advertised in the modern era without the use of the surrounding history that there is little image of Florida in the popular mind beyond one exclusively of playground.

In this nation of constantly homogenizing cultures, Florida's appeal to the imagination is, not surprisingly, stronger among non-Southerners. Southerners apparently don't really like Florida beach vacations. They have much the same brilliant sun as well as winters almost as short and mild. Having most of the same blessings lessens the need for an occasional Florida vacation. Besides, all but Tennessee and Kentucky have their own beaches. So more people from Michigan, as well as many other northern states, vacation in Florida than nearby Southerners. The result has been a tourist image devoid of regional or historical association, making of Florida a place that could exist anywhere near the water and sun. It isn't a Southern or even peculiarly American place to visit, but has become a tropical place of its own. Americans from elsewhere in the country and from other countries come in such numbers that Florida becomes for many a kind of hybrid, "a person or group of persons produced by the interaction or crossbreeding of two unlike cultures, traditions." But while hybridization is prized at garden nurseries, Pascua Hybridia has been far more helpful to those engaged in the tourist economy, than to the image of historical Florida. Lacking in the indelible images of Plymouth Rock, Independence Hall, the Shenandoah Valley, the French Quarter, or the Grand Canyon, Florida's image is vulnerable to the impression that it is all beach, only beach. The resulting irony is that in this oldest of places in America, millions of visitors retain the image of a place where the passage of time never occurred and may even not have been meant to be recorded. The Canadian chanteuse Anne Murray says she gives concerts in Florida because here she does not need to wear a watch.

A reputation more hybrid than Southern could have given Florida certain advantages, if the state could have ended up a composite of all the best of its visitors. San Franciscans read more books than Floridians. Seattleites keep their sidewalks cleaner. Bostonians support public radio and television more substantially, Cincinnatians maintain a better symphony. Somewhere in this country the citizens provide a better prison system, leave more trees in new developments, graduate a higher percentage of high school and college students, maintain better public parks, record lower infant mortality, recycle more resources, support charity more generously, and pay public servants better, among other characteristics of a society marked by a sophisticated cosmopolitanism. Florida has demonstrated a capacity for attracting visitors from all over the globe. Florida's appeal has not failed since first enticing European settlers here to cultivate olives and silk worms. If Florida is inevitably to be less Southern, more of an international hybrid, the resulting state would be better served by official advertising aimed at those who would commit their talents to the commonwealth, and less to those who contribute only retirement income and to the tourist economy. But that image does not result from the appeal of a theme park. The image of Florida is of a place of restless impermanence, a place without established traditional values. But as with so many other aspects of Florida, there is a wide gulf between the popular image and the real Florida. The antiquated, superannuated old silver square domed capitol in Tallahassee serves as one reminder of a very different Florida, quite the opposite of the familiar picture of endless transience. The old capitol is a reminder of the long years the government has operated from that same square in the middle of Tallahassee. Changed in outward appearance with the growing new state, it has been remodeled numerous times, beginning in 1824 and substantially rebuilt in 1845, 1902, when the dome was added, 1923, 1947 and, most irrevocably with a skyscraper, in 1977. But despite repeated attempts to shift it southward to accompany the march down the peninsula of the ever-increasing population, the capitol has from the beginning been in that same square in Tallahassee, and the 1845 building still sits in its accustomed place. The only more appropriate place for it might have been St. Augustine or Pensacola, the old capitals of East and West Florida. But they were too far apart for the only two metropolitan populations when time came to select one or the other; the moment for such a selection passed forever for both of Florida's first capitals, East and West, with the judicious choice of Tallahassee as the capital city for all Florida. Yet there is symmetry in that earlier and more reasonable, more image conscious era that the leaders during those years selected a site as nearly as possible exactly between the existing capitals at opposite ends of the northernmost edge of Florida, where it has remained from the beginning.

Georgians, in a state that has come to symbolize what is most solid about the nature of the Old South, have repeatedly moved their capital four times already, from Savannah to Augusta to Milledgeville and currently to Atlanta. With only a thirty-six year head start in the union, Georgia had moved its capital twice by the time Florida picked out Tallahassee. Virginians, often looked upon as the most traditional and established of Southern states, have nevertheless restlessly moved their capital from Jamestown to Williamsburg to Richmond. Alabama has moved its capital from Cahaba to Tuscaloosa to Huntsville and only finally to Montgomery. Those states sacrificed some individuality in the choice of a name of their capital city. There can surely be only one Cahaba, only one Milledgeville. There are a dozen Richmonds, Montgomerys, Columbias, even a dozen Atlantas. There is only one Tallahassee, though an Alabama town came close with a town name the same except for the "h." Only Baton Rouge can offer a distinctiveness equal to the original, the only name ever given to a capital of Florida, the state regarded by so many as ever restless, ever changing, ever paving over the old in an effort to upgrade for the sake of visitors. Florida, often regarded merely as the national seashore, which everyone including natives were expected to abandon at the end of the season, settled at the beginning once and for all on Tallahassee for its capital, despite a constant march of the population to the south since then, and occasional insurgencies to move it south.

At the time of the selection of a site for a capital in 1824, Pensacola had long been the capital of Old Spanish and British West Florida. St. Augustine had even longer been the capital of Spanish and British East Florida. Once the debate over entering the union as two separate states was settled in favor of one, satisfying abolitionists by controlling the number of potential slave-state senators, riders on horseback set out on the designated day moving toward each other from Pensacola and St. Augustine. They met at St. Marks on October 25, 1823, and two days later went on to the old Indian town of Tallahassee, literally "Old Town." There, halfway between the only two significant populations in 1824, they designated the capital of Florida, and so it has remained, in that one and only place, for one hundred seventy years, only thirty five years younger than Washington City as the national capital, itself having roamed from Philadelphia to New York before finally coming reluctantly to the banks of the Potomac, careful to remain on the north shore.

A capital not on the banks of a river may be part of Florida's failure to achieve the image of a place of unimaginably long standing. It is difficult to imagine the great capitals apart from their rivers. Paris is inseparable from the Seine, as London is from the Thames, Rome from the Tiber, Cairo from the Nile. Budapest, Belgrade, and Vienna all sit astride the Danube. America has followed that pattern almost without exception. Pierre, Bismarck, and Jefferson City all sit on the Missouri. Des Moines is on the Des Moines, and Santa Fe is on the Santa Fe. Harrisburg is on the Susquehanna, Hartford is on the Connecticut, Lincoln is on the Antelope, Boston is on the Charles, and Albany is on the Hudson. Topeka is on the Kansas, and Frankfort is on the Kentucky. Where possible, capitals are virtually on the sea: Olympia on Puget Sound, Providence on the Narragansett, Annapolis on the Chesapeake. With only a single exception, the paradigm of capitals astraddle rivers has been faithfully adhered to in the South just as in the rest of the world. Atlanta is on the Chattahoochee, Richmond is on the James, Baton Rouge is on the Mississippi, Montgomery is on the Alabama, Columbia is on the Saluda, Nashville is on the Cumberland, Raleigh is on the Neuse, Austin is on the Colorado, Frankfort is on the Kentucky, and Little Rock is on the Arkansas. Only Tallahassee among capitals in or near the South is not situated on the banks of a river, as though destined to be disenfranchised from the outset.

More than the topography carved by rivers was against John Lee Williams from Pensacola and William Hayne Simmons from St. Augustine, the two riders on horseback traversing the four hundred miles of North Florida in search of common ground for Florida's capital of the two united provinces of the old Spanish and British east and west Florida. Rivers do not flow down great stretches of the Panhandle or the Peninsula. The state isn't wide enough to provide for anything longer than the three hundred miles of the St. Johns, the longest river. There was simply no river conveniently located half way between Pensacola and St. Augustine, at least not one that would have permitted river traffic beyond Florida into Georgia or Alabama to the north. If political image makers had been in charge of the public perception of events in 1824, today's Tallahassee would doubtless be situated elsewhere. If today's presidential spinmeisters had been available to the designers of the first united Florida, surely they would have been foresighted enough gently to guide Simmons, coming from St Augustine in the east, to delay sufficiently long that Williams, coming from Pensacola in the west, could have covered more ground, in order that they might meet on a site nowhere else than on the banks of the Suwanee itself. As history's image is not in Florida's favor in 2000, history itself was not in 1824. The orders of the Legislative Council authorizing a capital selection site to be chaired by Zephaniah Kingsley was specifically directed to select a site north of St. Marks "between [not on] the Suwannee and Oclockany [Ochlocknee] Rivers," literally precluding a river bank capital. Only five miles more to the west would have situated the capital on the Ochlocknee; only ten miles south and it would have been on the Wakulla. If the absence of a capital city river is the disenfranchising circumstance, Tallahassee it nevertheless became. The historic seat of government was thought of as a lovely Southern village as long ago as 1876, when Sidney Lanier, seeing the capital only a decade after the ravages of war, still in the throes of Reconstruction, wrote in *Florida: Its Scenery, Climate, and History*, that "The repute of these people for hospitality was a matter of national renown before the war-and even the dreadful reverses of that cataclysm appear to have spent their force in vain against this feature of Tallahassee manners" (108).

But capital locations sometimes count for little. With all the great cities strung along California's coast, its capital is in none of them. Surely New York City was meant to be the state capital, as was New Orleans. Chicago is not the capital of Illinois, as Detroit is not the capital of Michigan. No one misguessed where the natural center of activity would ultimately be than Nevada. This century's mass of tourists might be forgiven for casually assuming Miami, or even Daytona Beach, to be Florida's capital. The last century might have guessed Jacksonville. The state's image could hardly have strayed any farther from its ancient origins if an earlier legislature had built a gleaming steel and glass condo-style capital overlooking Biscayne Bay. But there in Tallahassee it has sat for nearly two centuries, while all around it, across the panhandle to its east and west, up and down the entire length of the peninsula, Florida has literally exploded, its capital still firmly fixed in its original location, impervious to sea changes in population centers taking place elsewhere in Florida almost since Williams and Simmons first picked the old Indian village.

Its out of the way capital city notwithstanding, Florida's distinctive shape must have seemed the state's sure hope of an enduring image of importance and substance among the states. The elongated thrust of peninsula separating vast bodies of water, Atlantic from Caribbean, virtually creating the Gulf of Mexico, has lead each new wave of arrivals to want to push to the southernmost tip, just to see how it feels to go that far between the seas. Andrew Jackson didn't really like Florida, but he couldn't resist the notion of adding that incredible final extension of the coastline to America's already dramatic Atlantic shore. In arrogating Florida to the existing United States, he added to the national coastline the most noticeable feature in the entire distance from Nova Scotia to Dry Tortugas. Any other coastal feature becomes important only in terms of what has happened there. For instance, without the cities that have grown up there, the unimpressive coastal indentations where Boston, Manhattan, or Charleston came to be built would count for nothing to the eye but yet another inlet by comparison with Florida's dramatic seaboard, which would be even more noticeable without the cities. Florida's coastline was compellingly alluring even when it was thought to be inhabited only by savage Indians. James Madison wrote in 1803 to James Monroe that "the Floridas would inevitably be American soil one day because their position and the manifest course of events." It was an emotionally moving geography long before aerial views were possible, back even when it could only be imagined in a kind of mental Braille by sailing ever so tediously and slowly around it in clumsy galleons and caravels.

If Andrew Jackson had not added Florida to the distance of the United States, the two Henrys, Plant and Flagler, would have, eventually, or someone from the American entrepreneurial class like them. The building of serviceable railroads had been a goal in Florida well before the Civil War. But the lines that would extend to Florida make David Levy's original rail line from Fernandina to Cedar Key seem modest indeed. The builders of the great railroads would have found it unthinkable, perhaps even unAmerican, to lay rail lines all the way from Chicago or Boston to the St. Marys River, or to a more likely terminal at Jacksonville, or even all the way to Miami, and then stop, as though mere geography were a barrier to American industrial expansions. Plant and Flagler raced each other to get all the way to the end, when there was nothing there to go for but the going itself, building the most substantial travel tracks on the least expanse of land in the keys, barely separating the vast waters of the Atlantic and Gulf. That pace of expansion has not stopped since, throughout the entire twentieth century. In all that fast-paced, restless development, Florida's capital has been less influential in the tone of the changes than ideas imported by northern industrialists. Tallahassee sold the land cheap and had little to do with whatever development took place. The look of the stately old capitol has had little bearing on the texture of development in the six hundred miles to the south.

The human condition ordains birth, suffering, and death to be all that we each have in common. If there is anything everyone experiences within that, it is simply the weather. Everybody has weather. But of all things shared, weather is surety the lowest denominator. Yet since World War II that lowest common denominator has set the limits, the very definition of the popular image of Florida. One cannot imagine Juan Ponce de León or Hernando de Soto arranging their sailing or invasion schedules in order to arrive in Florida when their chain mail and wool underwear would be most suitable. Today's pioneers, by contrast, are not drawn to Florida because of love of land. They do not come even out of lust for gold and fortune. They certainly do not come to convert everyone to a love of a Catholic God. Today's new Floridians do not come even on the flimsy excuse of ancient legends of immortal youth. They come because the temperature is mild, and when the weather heats back up to its preternaturally essential level, they turn down the thermostats in their condos and mobile homes or they leave Florida to go home to cooler climes. A land once defined among Europeans by dreams of the impossible is now defined by its salubrious climate. New comers today cruise into Florida in airconditioned, window-tinted cars over the world's most invitingly smooth asphalt, right into parking lots next door to their rooms, convenience having completely redefined a land once accessible only to the most intrepid. With the departure of the ancient redoubtables, Florida became simply the nation's biggest sandbox, hardly the image envisioned by the original explorers.

But even when Florida was a destination only for the hardiest of travelers, it has always, since Ponce de León, been thought of as a place to go to temporarily, find something extraordinary, then go back home and—since the days of Jacques le Moyne in the 1560s—show others pictures so that they too might rave over it all. It has not much been thought of as a place to count the generations of one's own family. It should not surprise anyone that those who have numbered their generations here feel more like beneficiaries of an ongoing diaspora, rather than as inheritors of a place hallowed by the combination of antiquity in a wilderness setting.

Popular culture is now the ubiquitous source of information and value. But while popular culture has made universally known and admired heroes of rock stars, professional athletes, and network news-hour anchors, not even the ubiquity of popular culture has contributed anything to the image of Florida as a place with history and wild natural beauty. The movie-going public has thrilled to the exploits of tribes like the Apaches, Sioux, and Cherokees since the very earliest days of film making when Native Americans were still considered murderous savages. But no movie depicts the romance of the Timucuas, Tequestas, or Calusas defending life and limb in the pine barrens or the murky depths of Florida swamps. What Hollywood did for Geronimo on a windswept mesa, it did not do for him imprisoned in Fort Pickens, Pensacola, in 1886. What Hollywood did for a Sitting Bull triumphant at Little Big Horn, it never did for Seminoles crowding in palmetto thickets defending themselves against Andrew Jackson's raiding minions. Ask practically any student in the United States to name the site where an entire command of United States troops might ever have been wiped completely out by a band of savage indians and if he can answer at all, however strained his credulity in today's mood of superheated nationalism, he will say Little Big Horn, where Sitting Bull overcame Custer in 1876. That student will likely never have heard of Dade Battlefield, Sumter County, Florida, forty years before Little Big Horn, on that fateful December 28, 1835.

Outlaws of the old west slip easily into the popular culture of heroes on the basis of television and film. Films and songs about Osceola's capture beneath a flag of truce, or the treacherous taking and hanging of Ambrister and Arbuthnot under the flag of another country, or the destruction of old Negro Fort could have been the instruments of a far more widespread appreciation of Florida's difficult passage through the nineteenth century. Popular culture seldom conveys images of historical substance, but its almost universal popularity raises consciousness high enough to allow for the possible corrective re-examination, as in the less than universally acclaimed quincentenary of Columbus' landing in the New World. Why has the modern civil rights movement not made an icon of Zephaniah Kingley, a Jacksonville slave trader who married one of his slaves and willed her his entire holdings, only to have his last will and testament voided? How fortuitous for Florida's image in the struggle for civil rights had Stephen Spielberg turned for a subject to Kingsley rather than to the *La Amistad*. Sportsmen on steamboats laid waste to alligators and herons along the rivers of Florida every bit as wantonly and as completely as western cowboys did bison, but there has as yet been no display of American cowboy crassness decrying that less than sporting pastime, no "Dances with Alligators" featuring a Kevin Costner consciousness-raising role as Seminole rebel.

Florida enjoys beaches and sunshine so spectacular that they appear to overwhelm the possibilities for a more traditionally substantive Southern imagery. The words "Kentucky" and "bourbon" work together as reliably as "damn" and "yankee." Jack Daniels is synonymous with Tennessee, as Coca-Cola is with Georgia, or pralines with New Orleans. But neither "Minute Maid" nor "Tropicana" add much to the status of historical Florida in an image-conscious world. If John Gorrie had been an inventor-capitalist of the Industrial Revolution on the scale of Thomas Edison, then perhaps Gorrie, Inc., would be to Florida as Kellogg's is to Battle Creek, as Ford is to Detroit, Purina to St. Louis, Coca-Cola to Atlanta, or as Hershey is to Hershey.

The failure of Florida to achieve imagery for its history equal to that for its beaches repeats itself in many ways throughout the Florida milieu. Florida had over one hundred forty Spanish missions in place a century before California had any of its dozen, yet today, while everyone has heard of San Juan Capistrano, no one but professional archaeologists remember San Juan Potano. The unimpeachable legacy of the lasting architecture made possible in a later century in California affords the old missions there what mere wattle and daub deny to the historical missions of Florida, though they are older than the California sites. Because King Philip did not grant ownership of the land in Florida to the Spanish Franciscans, they had little encouragement to build in the permanent stone that has kept the king's own Castillo de San Marco intact two hundred fifty years. Reminders of their work exist in only two small remnants: shards of the foundation of San Luis de Apalache, at the confluence of the St. Marks and Wakulla Rivers, and the arches of Jororo and San

Antonio de Anacape, now part of the Turnbull sugar mill ruins in New Smyrna. The holy ground around Southern California's San Diego de Alcala probably beckons more today to Republicans than to pilgrims. On the other hand, a San Juan de Guacara built of what would have by now become ancient stone, on the Suwannee River, located in the Bible belt, might have proved a modern mecca. The custom of the Franciscans in Florida was to combine a saint's name with the name of the local tribe being ministered to. The result was mud chapels given such unlikely to be remembered names as San Mateo do Tolapatafi, San Pedro y Pablo de Potohiribi, Santa Maria de Los Angeles di Arapaha, San Cosme y San Damian de Cupaica, San Martin de Timucua y Ayacutun. But even in a bible belt society professing to hold religious values above all others, ancient sites where those values were first taught in the New World are forgotten. The more image-conscious Californians were clever enough to build beautiful stone and stucco chapels and give them such melodious names as San Juan de Capistrano. In California the names of the missions have continued in the California-lite tradition as names of vibrant, populous cities, such as San Carlos de Carmelo, whose mayors include Clint Eastwood, which has not proved a barrier to image building.

If history were just and equable, the Forbes Company of Apalachicola, or Panton, Leslie of Pensacola, would come as readily to mind as the East India Company, the Dutch East Indies Company, or Hudson's Bay Company when the heroes of the history of mercantilism are invoked. Those Florida trading companies had a great deal to do with the longest, costliest, and bloodiest Indian wars anywhere in the United States. A hundred years before Pocahontas immortalized

John Smith, Princess Ulelah saved Juan Ortiz from Hirrihigua in Tampa, but did not manage to confer on him the immortalizing imagery of the Virginia incident which Captain John Smith apparently plagiarized from the Floridians.

In an identical situation, Milly Francis rescued Duncan McKrimmon from Native Americans in the Florida Panhandle in 1818, but not even Florida schoolboys thrill to such romantic exploits. While the Pacific Northwest is easily brought to mind by the very mention of salmon, or New England with cod, Florida is evoked by either a non-edible, however glamorous sportsfish, the tarpon, or the fish, however delicious, nevertheless widely regarded in uninformed international cuisine as trash fish, the mullet. It is painfully emblematic of the failure of any image of Florida except sunny beaches that in the 1960s the state's fabled tourist advocacy agency, successful at bringing millions to Florida's beaches, failed in conducting a campaign to dignify the lowly mullet by popularizing it under its Spanish language name, the "lisa." Today, even Hispanics ask the fishmongers of Florida for mullet, not Lisa. Though Florida A & M University has had the second highest number of merit scholars of all predominately African American colleges, it is Fisk, Howard, Tuskegee, or Morehouse that come to mind when the crème de la crème among HBCUs comes up. Philanthropy makes it increasingly clear that the great institutions of higher education are perhaps the most valuable of all our cultural assets. But Florida has produced nothing that can be numbered among the great kudzu league of Southern universities. Florida spends its legacy on highways, yet Virginia's Blue Ridge Parkway, New Mexico's Santa Fe Trail, Mississippi's Natchez Trace, the old Federal Routes are the icons of the original

American instinct for roadbuilding, more so than the old Spanish Trail linking Pensacola and St. Augustine, older than any of the others, yet virtually uncelebrated anywhere in popular culture.

Florida glitters in the imagination of countless tourists. Probably as many people around the world have enjoyed the Florida sun and sand as have seen the longest-running ever Broadway musical, or read *Gone With the Wind*, or seen the Yankees play. But the powerful feel of the sun and the surf is not the source of images that give a state a substantial role in the long story of American culture, the five hundred years from earliest explorations of the New World to a position of absolute mastery among all the nations of the earth, the role of the super power of our time. When the sparkle of water and sand gives way to the reopening of school in the fall for all the summer visitors, little that defines the essential Florida remains in the popular imagination. Events in Florida history, of however much significance to the country, do not pass easily into the legends that inform us as a people. Ponce de León's discovery of the American mainland which, accurately or otherwise, is celebrated as the oldest of European events on these shores, becomes not a romance of heroic proportions but a tale of quixotic endeavor to find a Fountain of Youth, the stuff of children's fancies and fairy tales rather than the warp and woof of the myths capable of evoking the drama of national destiny. How fortuitous for Florida if Ponce de León's hopelessly romantic adventure to renew himself phoenix-like with a drink from the Fountain of Youth had struck more forcefully the imagination of the great Cervantes in search of a hero of his immortal story of innocent longing rather than the man of La Mancha that Cervantes gave to history. Cervantes was born only thirty-three years after Ponce de León discovered Florida. His *Don Quixote* was published just ahead of the centennial of de León's discovery. The same preference for the fanciful over the real is still borne out in Florida, the Fountain of Youth in 1513 giving way to Disney World in 1971.

In the writing and teaching of history, wars unfortunately always provide the defining moments. Among American school children perhaps only the French and Indian Wars could rival the Seminole Wars for last place in the recollection in history class. The Seminole Wars, most exacting of military conquests of Native American lands anywhere in America, occupies fewest pages in the text, fewest days devoted to lecture, smallest number of courses taught in the college history major's proscribed curriculum. It is as though the natural beauty of Florida were too stunning to imagine the extraordinarily long history, especially the unpleasant episodes, that have transpired in the long passage from 1513 to modern Florida.

In Statuary Hall in the United States capitol each state is represented by its choice of two of its own best. Other Southern states have installed likenesses of heroes whose names redound through all American history. Henry Clay, John C. Calhoun, Jefferson Davis, Huey P. Long, and Robert E. Lee in addition to George Washington stand there for the South, a pantheon of our best known and most honored. They all made their marks in politics or war, the surest routes to history. Virginia's history is so crowded with stellar figures from the Southern and American past that it does not need to call on the likes of Thomas Jefferson, or five of its other presidents, in order to name a worthy pair of Virginians. Florida is tellingly represented there not by a political office holder but, until recently, by Confederate General E. Kirby Smith, for one, and by Dr. John Gorrie, the inventor of air-conditioning, thus the real inventor of modern Florida, Ponce de León notwithstanding. In choosing General Smith, Florida risks comparison with the likes of Lee, Stuart, Longstreet, Pickett, or Beauregard, names familiar to most, as well as with the state's own more instrumental Joseph Finegan, who was defending Gainesville, Jacksonville, Olustee, and much of north Florida while E. Kirby Smith was presiding over the capitulation in Texas. Though losing his Fernandina home to confiscation by the army of occupation for an orphanage for children of former slaves, Finegan's popularity remained. Florida voters chose him to be in the first legislature to assemble during Reconstruction. In choosing Gorrie for the Washington rotunda, Florida chose its defining product, air-conditioning. But Florida's image as the site even of that ingenious invention gains nothing from the capitalist-consumer economy that bestows air-conditioning's benefits, since his name did not subsequently become synonymous with the product of his great imagination, as an automobile to many is a Ford, or Chrysler, rather than the abstract "auto." Had air-conditioning been invented by a Floridian named Carrier, or York, or the Crane of bathroom fixtures, or the Singer of sewing machines, Florida's role in that signal piece of Industrial Revolution history might enjoy a higher profile among the icons of American inventiveness. But Statuary Hall in the capitol notwithstanding, Florida gets no benefit to its image among states of the modern union for having provided the Dr. John Gorrie who did invent the most modern of miracles. No Floridian ever became a Southern icon in the same constellation with such familiar stars as Lee, Davis, Calhoun, Clay, or even, at another extreme end of that perspective, George Wallace, Lester Maddox, or Newt Gingrich, to say nothing of Sergeant York, Daniel Boone, or George Washington. Florida might have been put forth more splendidly by any one of the Spaniards, de León, de Avilés, de Vaca, de Soto, de Ayllón, de Luna. Our history might have provided itself a more lasting image to have been represented among the statues of the noteworthy by the perhaps only mythical, but nevertheless colorful pirate, José Gaspar, but Louisiana's Jean Lafitte is the pirate who became a famous hero, not Florida's Gaspar. Lafitte is in the biographical appendix of every modern English dictionary, but Gaspar is listed in none of them. In a world where blackguards are lionized in popular culture, and no one observes "famous" and "infamous" as linguistic opposites, neither Ma Barker nor even Florida's Mr. Watson, despite the efforts of novelist and travel-writer Peter Matthiessen, will likely any time soon be known as far and wide as Jesse James, Al Capone, or Bonnie and Clyde. Many of the South's stalwarts in Statuary Hall were known to have been slave owners, but even among slaveholders-traders surely Zephaniah Kingsley is noteworthy for having tried to dignify what used to be called miscegenation with legal marriage. Florida would surely have been equally well represented by the leaders of the warlike Seminoles, Micanopy, or Bowlegs, or the great Osceola. The vicissitudes of history have allowed few connections between outstanding Floridians and Florida's long history.

Florida's image is not burnished by a balcony from which the Marquis de Lafayette spoke; the renowned Frenchman never visited the vast tract of twenty-three thousand acres in Florida deeded to him in appreciation for his Revolutionary War exploits. Florida can claim no bedroom in which George Washington slept. Florida's defining image might have come from the vigor of the 1920s boom, an economic endeavor of phenomenal proportions. The boom left in its wake an art deco wash the length of South Beach that became one of Florida's few truly original contributions to serious art. But the decorative motifs of that all-too-brief bright light seem now to have had no more artistic influence than merely a smear across most of South Florida, paving the way for the glare of the neon version of Florida that soon followed. In the other states of the South, tourist attractions are not the opposite of all the state is or has been. Atlanta's Stone Mountain, Mobile's Bellingrath Gardens, North Carolina's New Bern and Virginia's Williamsburg, the timeless European ambience of New Orleans' French Quarter, bring a tourist attracted by how those scenes connect with the long reach of the past. But in Florida, tourist attractions are based on subjects far removed from anything natural to Florida or its ancient past: zoos filled with the animals of wildest Africa rather than the creatures of Florida, or acres of attractions appealing to memory no longer than film animation. Gas stations come in the shape of dinosaurs, diners in the shape of igloos. Florida, more than Madison Avenue, represents the triumph of advertising; visitors can be convinced of wanting to see or do anything. But do so many come to Florida who don't actually want to see Florida? All of this is a long way from the old square-domed capitol rising above a square of live oaks. The destinations in Florida popular with millions are buttressed, reinforced by beaches designed to permit no hint of Florida's collective memory.

The multitude of first magnitude springs still boil enough crystal clear water to the surface to suggest the pristine Florida of the Pleistocene era. There is sufficient knowledge of the pre-de Leónian past to make Florida pre-eminent among sites of the aboriginal world of America. Enough coquina went into the building of the still-standing Castillo de San Marco to bring Florida to mind first among the landing sites of the age of exploration and discovery. Florida is draped in enough Spanish moss for the state to be able to take its rightful place among the states of the Old South. John Deering's home, Vizcaya, and John Ringling's Cà d'Zan are sufficient to remind the world of an imaginative early twentieth century boom Florida. Disney World brings the tally of the ages up to date. But unlike the remains of those earlier ages, the mentality surrounding this most recent part of the image of Florida threatens the existence of the remnants of those earlier ages. The celebration of these assets will be the measure of the age at hand in Florida.

1996

3

La Florida: Spanish Origins in an Anglicized World

Before Columbus claimed the New World, or Ponce de León named Florida twenty years later, medieval cartographers knew little of the shape of that early sixteenth-century old world they inhabited, and of course virtually nothing of the New World. But with each new moment of the great age of exploration and discovery, their maps began slowly to take definitive shape, proclaiming for their respective monarch-patrons vast tracts they would call Nouvelle France, Nueva España, Niuw Nederlands, or New England. But before any of these names were added to the maps, the New World that would become North America was known largely by the first name given to it, La Florida. It must have been bitter gall to the later Anglo-Saxon Americans busy forming the new nation of the United States to have to work with early maps of the New World showing the entire vast continent, stretching from Atlantic to Pacific, from Caribbean up to Nova Scotia, called, simply, La Florida.

It would not take many years for Martin Waldseemüller's 1508 map's perhaps wrongful misapplication of Amerigo Vespucci's name to the whole New World, thus disenfranchising Christopher Columbus in the naming of the New World, yet it nevertheless remains that among some early map makers neither "America" nor "Columbia" was the word. Nor was the word for this new world "Leonia," as it might more justly have been. It was, instead, all known poetically as La Florida. Had the Spaniards and the Spanish language maintained their original dominion throughout the New World through subsequent eras of colonization toward permanent political settlement, this new world might today be known by the name of Los Estados Unidos de America, but it might just as likely be known as Los Estados Unidos de la Florida.

The commencing of long sweeps of history sometimes turns on moments which might have appeared less than earth-shaking. In the northernmost reaches of the New World, General Wolfe prevailed against General Montcalm on the Plains of Abraham in one small battle that would make all of Canada, with the exception of Quebec, English. In the South, General Oglethorpe won the Battle of Bloody Marsh in Georgia, with a mere thirty-eight soldiers, ending Spain's hopes of extending an actual empire of Florida northward. Mexico's Santa Ana ultimately lost all of Texas even after initially overcoming the tiny Alamo. Thomas Jefferson made English lingua franca west of the Mississippi with fifteen million dollars and the Louisiana Purchase. The purchase of New Amsterdam transformed it into New York. Though Dutch and French interests competed in the beginning, it was Spanish effort and influence that was the earliest to become widespread and must once have seemed irresistible. Yet the authority with which English interests ultimately prevailed as the New World began five hundred years ago to take shape offers a precursory glimpse into our own time, in which the influence of English has established itself throughout the world as the language of commerce and diplomacy.

The relentless process of Anglicization that has been an underlying but always present theme of the history of the New World since 1607 remedied—some would say corrupted—that perceived mispronunciation, FlorEEda, to the present Anglicized FLORida, even as the same linguistic juggernaut was transforming the original "el legarto" into the very Anglo-American beast known ubiquitously today as the alligator. The name "el legarto" is itself a measure of the extent to which Spanish replaced the aboriginal languages of Florida, where that rough beast was earlier known as "allapattah," from the original Creek-Seminole, a name that might just as judiciously have entered modern history. It was doubtless a torturous route of mispronunciation, one that could speak volumes about the people of the early New World, that accompanied the cracker route from "el legarto de la Florida" slowly and painfully to Florida alligator, hence relentlessly on down to today's sound-byte sized "gator."

In 1519, just six years after Ponce de León's creation of what was then known as La Florida, Hernán Cortés astonished the Old World by conquering the Aztec empire, establishing a Spanish language empire in Nueva España that would endure. It must have seemed that Mexico would always enjoy its claims to a history prior to anything the English or French could match in what would come to be known as North America, though no one then could have imagined that Mexico would ever take its place as the largest Spanish-speaking nation on earth. Mexico still reveals scenes of pre-conquest people, country, and languages at every turn; a Mexico long before it was Spanish or Catholic. There is very little trace of what the U.S. was before the Anglo-Saxon Protestant conquest. Only in place names does pre-English America survive.

What Cortés had done in Mexico, Pizarro would second in Peru just ten years later, to add to Spain's early domination in the New World. If Spain could succeed on such a scale, it must have seemed inconceivable that there would ever be a threat to the Spanish language in the New World. The whole vast sea around which Nueva España revolved quite fittingly became known as the Gulf of Mexico. Ponce de León having preceded Cortés, that great sea might just have easily become known as the Gulf of Florida. Either way, Spain and Spanish ruled. The process of applying names that would endure doubtless favored Mexico because of the abundance there, as opposed to the bitterly disappointing absence in Florida, of gold. The vast reserves of Aztec and Incan gold are no longer available to the Spanish treasury, but the Spanish treasury of language, however much Anglicized in pronunciation, remains. That sea around which all of the glamorous activity revolved was Spain's to call the Mexican Sea, just as it was Spain's to call the "gulf."

But despite the long-lived Spanish invention of the "Gulf of Mexico," English replaced Spanish thoroughly elsewhere. Florida place names reflect dozens of such changes. It is a little surprising that the nautical nomenclature of the Gulf was not altered to the Anglo-Saxon equivalent, as happened so often in other instances. In that case the Gulf might have become the Bay of George II, or the Georgian Sea or, had a persuasive old Scotsman been aboard and in a position of authority, the Firth of George. If English had actually prevailed at the naming of the Gulf of Mexico, however, it might just as easily have become known by an even older Anglo-Saxon term for bay, sea, or lagoon, namely, a "bight," which was the fate of several indentations of the Florida coast. The Bight of Mexico. The Bight of Florida. War is history, but only for the winners. The language of the winner is the ultimate maker of history, which in turn is inherited by all the generations to come. There is today on the Florida coast, flowing into the same Gulf of Mexico, a number of "indentations or curves in shore or sea, as a bay, or bend," and among them several actually did acquire that early Anglo-Saxon etymon for bay, a "bight," as in the naming of the Bight of Santini, the Bight of Rankin, and the Bight of Garfield. Irresistibly, one might imagine, English influence also left behind on the Florida coast an indentation known today as "Snake Bight." That level of imagination could easily have endowed the present with a "Bight of Mexico," once English asserted itself in the long sweep of history, however unlikely such a geographical place name seems after so many eras of calling that body of water the Gulf of Mexico. Another English language conquest, Australia, has a gulf on its northern shore linguistically balanced by having a bight on its southern shore.

The modern ear, familiar now for centuries with a "Gulf of Mexico," shudders at the narrowly averted Bight of Mexico, or lumbering Spanish galleons catching the swift currents of the Bight Stream up the Atlantic coast before striking across the ocean for Spain, or today's Bight States as a distinct part of the South, or the beautiful beaches of the Bight Shore, or the Bight Islands National Seashore. Those inlets of Florida which did come to be called by the Anglo-Saxonism "bight" are on the lower southwest coast. The last area of Florida to be explored and named, less developed still today than most coastal areas, the southwest has largely been rescued from the inroads of development by the Everglades National Park. In that vast area of the state, the most remote areas of otherwise bustling, metropolitan Florida, the use of the term "bight" enhances the atmosphere of a landscape unchanged after centuries of European languages. In the more developed areas of the Florida coast to the north of the Everglades, names are more apt to occur in combination with the customary Anglicization of "bay," as Tampa Bay, or harbor, as in Charlotte Harbor. That predominantly English nomenclature prevails elsewhere along the coast except in the old northwest of Florida, the Pensacola territory, where one is drawing close to New Orleans and the remnant influence of France. The operative geographical terminology there is not bight or harbor but, predictably, bayou. No Saxon bights or French bayous surface on the glitzier east coast of Florida, the famous gold coast, despite the Anglicization of that coast. Bight might have been the word once, but it is not nearly modern enough to suffice for a modern Palm Beach on the shores of a waterway called Snake Bight. Farther south, Collins Avenue would be considerably less upscale, more cumbersomely old fashioned had it terminated at what had come to be known as Biscayne Bight.

The early predominance of Spanish in the naming of geographical features might have resulted in the inclusion on today's maps of Florida many places not called bay or bight or bayou but called bahia, the Spanish for bay. Only Bahia in Brevard County, tiny Bahia Oaks west of Ocala, and Bahia Hondo Key maintain what was once a flourishing habit of bestowing the designation of bahia. Pensacola Bay was first named Bahia Filipina del Puerto Santa Maria in 1559 by Tristán de Luna, in honor of King Philip and the Virgin Mary. It was rechristened Bahia de Santa Maria de Galve in 1693 by Admiral Pez, in honor of the Virgin and the Conde de Galve, viceroy of New Spain. Bahia Biscayne, or even Bahia de Mexico, would have come to be as comfortable as any bay, bayou, gulf or bight.

The namer of the Gulf was under the sway not of Shakespeare's English but of the earlier more literary Italian "golfo," derived from the Old French "golfe" both from elegant Greek "kolpos," for bosom, lap. The namer of the Gulf of Mexico was not charmed either by the Old English "bight," from Dutch "bocht," from German "bucht," for bend, or bay. The fervent Floridist might still wish that the long historical process of nomenclature had delivered down through the ages to us not the Gulf of a foreign name like Mexico, but the Gulf of Florida, the three successive dental fricative f's rubbing against each other, hissing a name that would push familiarity with the name of Florida even farther out across the globe of the world found in every school room in the world. The Straits of Florida would then provide the only outlet from the Gulf of Florida to the Caribbean and on to the Atlantic. One might even be willing for that vast inland sea, so much a part of the history of Florida, to have been a Bight, if it could have been the Bight of Florida. Waldseemüller seems less intransigent in light of the exigencies of linguistic history and dominion since.

But the name "Mexico" obtained, as did Gulf, and so it is still named, perhaps prophetically. The Spanish, once in possession of virtually all of the New World, are perhaps now, after centuries of eclipse in this hemisphere, once again finding reason to rejoice. The growing Hispanic presence, and consequently the linguistic hegemony of Spanish all the way around the Mexican Gulf, no longer just at the southern tip of the crescent, is now obvious. From the Yucatan up through Galveston and on around to New Orleans, old Spanish glories dot that curving shore here and there where Spanish priests and conquistadors once ruled, having left behind a legacy of place names scattered all the way down to Key West, once Cayo Hueso.

Texas and California undergo re-Hispanicization today as much or more than Florida, yet Florida has a special role to play in the influence of Spanish once again expanding in the new world. There was never a whole new world called by either of the names of Texas or California. There was, on the other hand, once a world known, if only briefly, as La Florida. So pride of place in the New World should go to Florida, preeminent among states of the union, having been the first colony, having once had its name applied to all then known of the New World of North America.

Such was not to be the case. Few evolutionary processes illumine the biases of history more than etymology, sweeping along with it all of history's attendant prejudices. On May 29,

1586, Sir Francis Drake, most romantic of Queen Elizabeth's courtiers, downgraded himself to pirate, pillaging and burning St. Augustine. He acquired little treasure there to add to the plunder he had already robbed from Spanish galleons to present to the Virgin Queen upon his return to London. But history continues to be as revealingly cruel as Francis Drake's piracy; had there been a Boston, New York, Philadelphia or Baltimore for Drake to burn, every schoolboy of a certain generation in the United States would likely have had to read about that raid. That schoolboy might even have been required to learn some mnemonic jingle memorializing the event. But St. Augustine is Floridian, Southern, and Spanish, whichever of the three origins has most offended the steady pace of the Americanization and Anglicization of New World history, thus relegating the event to the role of mere footnote in the proper credits of the steadily accreting annals of the nation-to-be. *The World Almanac and Book of Facts 1996*, in its chronological outline of world history, gives for the single event of consequence throughout the new world in 1565 this ominously conclusive report: "St. Augustine, Florida, founded by Pedro Menéndez de Avilés. Razed by Francis Drake in 1589." As though it were no more. Today forty-five million people a year hurry past the St. Augustine site of that raid four hundred years ago, on their way to Disney World, completing the process of fashioning the national character by replacing history with entertainment. Twentieth-century uses of history require none of the sterner correctives of the past. It is perhaps a more fortunate circumstance than first realized that the history which Karl Marx warned would keep us enslaved has dissolved, even without his economic system enabling the revolution.

45

Both history and etymology always belong to victors. American history reads as though the *Mayflower* were the flagship of a mighty armada of ships that saved the new world from its unlettered aborigines and from the rest of Europe. Historians even of Florida's past seldom if ever celebrate the moment of discovery by reciting the minutiae that renders such a moment unforgettable. So not even historians of Florida ceaselessly repeat the name of the ship, the *Nuestra Señora de Santiago*, that brought Ponce de León to Florida in 1513, as American historians recite the name *Mayflower* as a talisman making the New World safe for English. Nor do historians of America or of Florida recite the name of the ship in which Pánfilo de Narváez arrived in 1528, or Hernando de Soto's *San Cristobal de San Juan* in 1539. Tristán de Luna's thirteen ships and 1,500 men arrived in Pensacola in 1559 virtually unnamed, according to historians, making less of a mark on history than the one small *Mayflower* has made even on the most scrupulously accurate chroniclers of the New World. De Luna's voyage to Pensacola was seconded by a voyage by Ángel de Villafañe in 1561, arriving behind de Luna with 60 people aboard four ships, but to no particular place in history. Jean Ribault's *Trinite* sailed up the St. Johns in 1562 at the head of a flotilla of six more ships, but to little historic fanfare for the *Trinite*, as did René de Laudonnière in 1564, or Pedro Menéndez de Avilés' *San Pelayo*, followed by eight more ships, in 1565 to found St. Augustine. History's selectivity is not confined just to Florida's past, but so many of the very earliest voyages of the great age of exploration occurred in Florida that these earliest makers of Florida should account for more attention in an age that prides itself on scientifically accurate historiography. Bartholomew Gosnold arrived in

Jamestown in 1607 on the *Godspeed*, the *Discovery*, and the *Susan Constant*, but not to much acclaim by Yankee historians. Henry Hudson arrived in New York on the *Half Moon* in 1609. Lord Baltimore's crew arrived in the Chesapeake in 1634 aboard the *Ark* and the *Dove*. William Penn arrived on the Delaware River in 1682 aboard the *Welcome*. General James Oglethorpe arrived in 1733 on the *Ann* to found Savannah, but Georgia students seldom if ever hear of it. Yet custom and convenience allow all of that to come down to just the one easy ship, the *Mayflower*. In the relentless Anglicization of the New World radiating in unceasing waves out from Harvard Yard and the historians there to whom pride of place gave primacy if not completeness in the telling of the story of America, none of these Spaniards, Frenchmen, or the Englishmen who became Southerners rather than Bostonians have been able to convey on their ships or their deeds the kind of history that would live in instant recognition. But if history is capricious, irony may perhaps be as well, the *Mayflower* signaling the shortest lived of seasons and blossoms. In the fullness of time, for which revisionist history must wait, the Hispanicization of the South and West may offer the corrective to the histories and perhaps even the etymologies that until now have given Boston, or even Jamestown, but never St. Augustine, the blue ribbon for coming in first.

Florida is denied the role its longevity properly ordains for it in both Anglophilic and, simultaneously, Hispanophobic America. Yet it is once again the tandem ceremony of history and irony that bequeaths Florida its most noticeably unSouthern legacy, the snowbirds of Yankee retirement. It is after all not the conquistadors of Old Spain, or their monk-priests who struggled to Christianize Florida, who turned out to be progenitors of Florida's most ubiquitous complainers. The most despised of all species, the damyankee, owes its dubious origins to the pious Anglo-Saxon Protestants who came first on the *Mayflower*, settled in Boston and New York and all points west only to transmogrify into a horde of twice-invading Yankees who now very nearly own the entire peninsula of Florida. England, France, and Spain all tried to own and possess Florida, but would never put it first among possessions with the necessary men and materiel to hold and so lost it. Spain traded Florida to England for a mere Cuba in 1763, though the House of Commons attacked the exchange of the more significant trading site of Cuba for what was then known as the territory of mere West Florida, a tract extending from the Apalachicola River halfway across the Florida Panhandle and then west to Natchez, Mississippi. England traded Florida back to Spain for a mere Bahamas twenty years later, in 1783. Neither of them took proprietorship of Florida seriously. Governors of Florida were Spanish when Spain was the enemy of the new United States; governors of Florida were British when Britain was the enemy of the United States.

Nor did America put Florida first among its acquisitions. President James Monroe's cabinet left abundant record that their only reason for trying to steal Florida was to keep Britain or Spain from possessing it. That was not a cabinet made up of egregious sycophants, either, who might have been expected to agree with President Monroe on virtually any topic. John C. Calhoun, fiery South Carolinian with presidential aspirations of his own and very nearly the means to carry them out, was the Secretary of War who went along with Monroe's unworthy ambitions for Florida. No less a thinker than John Quincy Adams, future president and son of a president, was there as Secretary of State and certainly knew the ramifications of what President Monroe was doing by the attempted theft of Florida. William Crawford, who probably should himself, abler than Monroe, have been president, sat on that cabinet as Treasurer. These were not men without an overview of the consequences of history. If President James Monroe had any historical ambition for Florida, it was only in the hope that its acquisition by whatever means would rank his virtual theft of Florida with his predecessor Jefferson's more legitimate purchase of Louisiana. Only Andrew Jackson ever concentrated long enough or with sufficiently intense vitality to accomplish its final conquest, and his only reason for doing so was not love of Florida but his hatred of the three European powers who wanted it and the Native Americans who deserved it.

Failing the hurricane that would sweep the peninsula clear of all those who have claimed it as their own for yet a new effort at ultimate settlement, Florida remains suspended as it always has been, except that it now finds itself awaiting a new Hispanicization of America as African-Americans give way as the largest minority among Americans. Those today who would order the drawbridge up by forbidding signage in Spanish, or double ballots, or even a foreign language requirement of America's already woefully xenophobic students, cannot claim ignorance of history on their side. We should know better by now.

This oldest yet newest place in the New World waits for the Spanish language to come once again into its own. The historical timeline revealed in the process of giving names to geographical locations in Florida shows Spanish influence kept at bay in favor of a possibly even less likely source of names, those of the aboriginal population. Cities, much older than counties, bear native names such as Ocala, Tampa, or Miami, though they might, if named later, have been called after the appropriate Spanish explorers. The creation and naming of counties is a phenomenon of a later stage of American politics, well after the arrival of an English model of governance, and reveals the attendant prejudices of those later, English-speaking generations. Governors and Presidents and even the abstractions of Dixie and Liberty have thus taken precedence over the Spanish past in modern political nomenclature. George Washington was not first but third in line in Florida to be honored in 1825 with a county in his name, thirty years after his presidency. Florida's intransigence is measured in naming a county for Andrew Jackson, also in 1822, six years before he ever became president. James Monroe was in the eighth year of his presidency, when he was honored in 1823, Madison in 1827, fifteen years after his, Jefferson in 1827, twenty years after his, Taylor not until 1856, six years after his. Polk, the last president honored in Florida with a county bearing his name, was fifteen years out of office and the last to be so honored, coming as his honor did in 1861, when Florida ceased honoring presidents of the union.

The entire process of creating and naming counties ceased with the interruption of Civil War and did not commence again for twenty-five years, when it resumed with long-overdue sympathy for Florida's native past in the naming in 1887 of Osceola County, though Seminole County did not come into being until 1913, near the end of the creation of new counties whose names might honor the long past. Micanopy is the perfect name for the jewel of a town that it still is. With the revival of creating and naming counties after the

Civil War, Florida turned its attention to other native sons, usually its more nearly homegrown governors. The characteristically Anglo-Saxon quality of Florida's early mood has exhibited itself in naming the third of sixty-seven counties for Andrew Jackson, while he was still governor of the territory, though he was not actually in Florida, having already given it up to return to Tennessee. William Pope Duval was similarly honored in 1822 while still governor. Then the century of the presidential honors passed before Napoleon Bonaparte Broward was honored in 1915 with his own county six years after his tenure. Albert W. Gilchrist in 1925 had been out of office seven years, Cary Hardee in 1921 four years, and John S. Martin still in his first year of office when honored in 1925 by a county in his name. Hernando de Soto assists most impressively in correcting the absence of early Spanish notables by accounting for not one but two counties, plus Leon and Santa Rosa. But the absence of many Spanish place names continues as a historical oddity across the state. San Pablo worked its way circuitously into Sampala. Though there is a St. Petersburg, there is no San Pedro. Marion County's tiny Pedro did not make it into either of the standard references, Allen Morris's *Florida Place Names* or Bertha Bloodworth's *Places in the Sun*.

Southern and American Hispanophobia may not be the real roadblock in Florida's long evolutionary path toward either full participation in Anglo-Saxon America, or parity with New England by virtue of its long Spanish past. Florida's problem may be simply jealously, that La FlorEEda was already old when the balance of this vast country got underway, that Florida has its roots in a Spain and Spanish culture already on the wane in Europe when Florida began. The Spanish Armada, intended by King Philip to be captained by none other than Pedro Menéndez de Avilés, sank only twenty years after Menendez founded St. Augustine. Whatever the source of discomfort of Spanish origins in an English world, Florida still feels like a place waiting to happen, an as yet immature place in an otherwise very old-seeming Old South. A state crowded mainly by transients feels remarkably like the earliest Florida must have felt, the battleground between contending English, French, aboriginal, cracker, Seminole and Spanish forces all struggling their way to ultimate possession.

First published in *Southern Studies: An Interdisciplinary Journal of the South*, XIII:I-II (Spring/Summer 2006), 105-113.

4

Florida History:
The Most Difficult American Birthing

If there were a single sphere in which Florida might have expected its image to shine forth among the states it would surely be the role conferred upon a place by a long history. Yet in standard textbook accounts of American history, the discovery and colonization of Florida by Spaniards is at most a kind of romantic footnote. In the venerable Oxford Companion series, famous for accuracy, the companion to American history reports that Ponce de León was "mortally wounded by Seminole Indians" (643), though there were no Indians who went by that name for nearly three hundred years after the death of Ponce de León. Cursory accounts of early Florida in much American history provide little more than a means of holding the unfolding of the history of Florida in abeyance until it became a part of the English-speaking union three hundred years after that history began.

The history of a place becomes widely important only after that place achieves economic, political, or even cultural dominance. Britain's long history would be less well observed had Britain not conquered half the world in the nineteenth century, and perhaps not even then if the English language had not completed its conquest of the earth in this century. The history of a minor player on the world stage like, say, Pakistan is more significant to the origins of society because of its length than that of many nations of greater economic consequence. Much of the origins of civilization comes from Mohenjo-Daro in the valley of the Indus River. But that history has had little influence in a world in which Pakistan has remained only a minor player. So it has been with Florida.

Florida's recorded history is the longest of all the areas that would become states, but its long history has not given its image the place at center stage that sometimes derives simply from the circumstance of an extraordinarily long, colorful, event-filled history. Florida remained a sparsely populated frontier during the three hundred years the rest of the eastern United States was taking political shape. After becoming a territory and then a state, its political importance has been until recently relatively minor. One proposal before the Reconstructionist Congress following the Civil War was to remove to Florida all of the slaves freed in the other states of the South. That use of Florida would not have been in deference to the salubriousness of its famous climate. Indifference to Florida's antiquity is borne out in its image as a temporary vacation from the real world. The state of millions of residents and a huge state budget made possible by a mammoth tourist industry is a recent phenomenon. Until recently, Florida was more on the fringe of events than is suggested even by its unusual peninsular geography. Its history colluded in separating it from a role in the main events of the rest of the Atlantic seaboard. Florida's origins belong to a Spain that ceased to be a major player on the world stage at the time the United States took shape. Spanish is Mediterranean, Latin, and Catholic, and was distastefully foreign-seeming to most early Anglo Americans. The prevailing tone in the eastern United States except Florida has from the beginning been Northern European, Germanic, and Protestant. All of this combines to isolate Florida in a manner that has denied the status its unequalled longevity might otherwise bestow.

If Florida had become home to a larger population as early as the states of the northeast, or if it had been home to the giants of the Industrial Revolution, or even if it had been home to a small number of the volatile, firebrand personalities who led the way to the wars and elections and newspapers of early efforts at independence from Britain, Florida history would have achieved more commanding appreciation, perhaps bringing not only its European but also its pre-Columbian past to more attention. The first historians to write about a place tend to set a tone that is difficult to change later, even after more actual facts about the place come to light. That is particularly true if the earlier historians, however incomplete or even inaccurate their accounts, were nevertheless graceful, persuasive writers, claimed prestigious academic addresses, and were published by highly respected presses. After the passage of many years, their books have been handed down as texts through enough succeeding generations of teachers and students to have achieved the status of authorized opinion. When the version of American history that became official was taking shape in the early years of massed-published history texts, those historians possessed all three advantages. They were good writers at prestigious universities and were published by respected presses, all of which has combined to sanction their having overlooked any significance of events in early Florida. Moreover, they were notably Anglophilic, even during a time when the young America was striving to assert complete cultural independence from Britain. And if English America was conflicted over separating itself from England, how much greater the conflict for Florida, by that time American, having to separate itself from Spanish origins.

Those early academic writers of the history of the United States doubtless bristled dismissively in discussing a place like Florida that had for almost all of the previous three hundred years pledged allegiance to rulers in such places as Havana, Veracruz, and Mexico City, rulers who were themselves mere viceroys to the real rulers in Madrid. But Havana was an important European site before any other location in North America, and Florida was in its orbit. The Caribbean had been the site of Columbus' landfall; one result of his discovery was the Pope's dividing line through the earth. Spain took early command of efforts to rule all of the New World. Havana was the center of the Spanish West Indies and from it all exploratory activity radiated. It was the earliest center of the New World, to which everyone gravitated then as surely as today's financiers to Wall Street, aspiring playwrights to Broadway, or world leaders to Washington. As difficult as it was for an earlier generation of Americans to countenance governance from what they regarded as foppish, effete London authorities, the idea of governance of anything American from decadent, Catholic Madrid or its colonial offspring Havana would have been for the historians of that era unseemly if not unthinkable. The American model of the hero, already evolving from the rugged frontiersman on its way to the Marlborough man, dismissed the elaborate European manners of men in wigs, satin knee pants, and silver shoe buckles, especially if they spoke Spanish. Hispanophobic resentment centering on Havana did not end with the 1821 cession of Florida to the United States, but continued beyond even the 1898 Spanish-American War on up to the present hostility toward Fidel Castro's Communist regime. When the long history of Florida comes to mind for many, the absence of any association with more easily remembered events such as the Boston Tea Party, the Continental Congress, the Revolutionary War, or any of the events surrounding the first nine presidential elections in American history leaves only a sketchily recalled association with Spain, to this day not the favorite ally of the United States. It probably did not serve well the image of Florida's history among an earlier generation of historians that "adelantado of Florida" was still among the titles accruing to the numerous honorifics belonging to the distinguished de Avilés family.

Widespread familiarity attaches to only very small moments of history. Centuries of native history, plus the convoluted French versus English attempts at colonization, become crystallized for the average American in the landing at Plymouth. It has been comfortable to the teaching of American history for the Pilgrims to have had reassuringly familiar English names, to be captained by men without aristocratic titles in foreign languages, unlike the Spanish conquistadors whose efforts were diminished even by the mispronunciation of their names. History favors the simplest answers, and the Pilgrims obliged by sailing on a single ship with an easily pronounceable English word for its name, that word not even the name of some titled Englishman but of a very ordinary, everyday object. Not even English names of ancient sounding origin came into favor until the arrival of suburban housing developments. Christopher Columbus was, luckily for his place in America's economic version of history, not an aristocratic Spanish don with a name trailing "y's" and "de's," but even his three ships might not have survived history's economies so readily had he not been accorded first place among explorers. But he is universally regarded in popular history as having been the discoverer. Leif Ericson and John Cabot are usually at least mentioned in the opening accounts of American history but with only the kind of apologetic backward-looking comment thought to serve only to retard the easy flow of history, history class lectures, even history texts. Pánfilo de Narváez and Cabeza de Vaca don't even get that. Ponce de León obliged none of those economies of the mind of the historian but, with characteristic Hispanic fervor, sailed on ships with names too un-English to remember with comfort, the *Santa Maria de la Consolacion*, the *San Cristobal de San Juan,* and the *Santiago.* Illustrating the purposes popular history is made to serve, the most recently published dictionary of American English gives for the entry "Santa Maria" not the name of the Mother of God but "the flagship used by Columbus when he made his first voyage of discovery to America in 1492." For "Santiago," it cites the capital of Chile, but not the pilgrim shrine of Spain, or the flagship of Ponce de León.

Hernando de Soto, for all the riveting accounts of discovery he made available, was even less respectful of the exigencies of historical simplicity by arriving on nine ships, with the difficult names of the *San Cristobal*, the *La Magdalena*, the *La Concepcion*, the *Buena Fortuna*, the *San Juan*, the *Santa Barbara*, and three others nameless even among careful historians. Pedro Menéndez de Avilés cannot even by historians in something of a hurry avoid mention for having established the first successful European city here. He arrived aboard the *San Pelayo*, with the *San Andres*, the *San Salvador*, the *Holy Ghost*, *Our Lady of the Rosary*, the *Sant Antonio*, *La Victoria*, *La Esperanza*, and the *San Miguel* in tow, a fleet Catholic and complicated compared to the ease of a single *Mayflower*. To the average American, if not the average teacher of American history, these antique and foreign sounding names, arriving in a country determined to separate church and discovery, might as well have been the names of space ships from galaxies far away. For the average consumer of history, the *Mayflower* summons up and carries with it all that need be known of a hundred or more years of early New England history, consuming Florida's in the process.

It is not a crime not to know the history of a particular province, even if one is native to that province. Americans are better known for indifference to provincial lore than for passion for it. An important lesson from the experience of environmentalists and historic preservationists, though, is that widespread familiarity with and appreciation for the history of a place offers a kind of sanctity useful in saving historic sites from the blight of development. The events of the Continental Congress will not save downtown Philadelphia from urban decay, but general familiarity with that history must change to some extent how business is done there. Proximity to Independence Hall and the Liberty Bell must make a more circuitous path to a franchise next door for Taco Bell. Disney World did not get permission to build across the highway from Manassas battlefield. City fathers looking for the cheapest way to modernization must usually be more mindful of a history that is widely acknowledged and celebrated. Disney World did get permission to build across the street, virtually, from some of the fiercest stands Seminoles made against invading American armies, and that permission having once been granted, nothing has prevented the continual sprawl outward of that site and all its attending blight. Perhaps only poverty and neglect favor history. St. Augustine might today look very much like Miami, leaving nothing of the ancient city, if the railroads had not shifted general interest southward almost immediately after making their way as far south as Florida, allowing largely under populated somnolent north Florida to sleep awhile longer into the twentieth century, long enough at least for an interest in history to catch up with an expanding economy.

History favors the neat, crisp economy of such a moment as Bunker Hill, or the "rude bridge that arched the flood," over the years of clandestine, duplicitous machinations of James Madison, James Monroe, George Mathews, Andrew Jackson and others attempting to wrest Florida from Spain without having to wage open war for it. After the bright shining moment of discovery at Pascua Florida in 1513, few moments in Florida history have been characterized by anything near the exactness of Ponce de León's moment in the Florida sun. The inexact course of the Creek Civil War, the War of 1812, the Seminole Wars, or the juggling trade-offs between England and Spain, subsequent to unfamiliar wars like the French and Indian, whereby England got Florida from Spain, the loser, or even the American Revolution, whereby Spain got it back from England, the loser, leave early Florida without the images that make history easily memorable—moments such as the Star-Spangled Banner, Valley Forge, or Shiloh. Where in popular history is Wahoo Swamp, the Cove of the Withlacoochee, Payne's Prairie, Moultrie Creek? All of the voyages of Ponce de León, Tristán de Luna de Ayllón, Pánfilo de Narváez, Pedro Menéndez de Avilés, Hernando de Soto, and Jean Ribaut do not carry along with them the power of instant recognition and familiarity of the *Mayflower* landing at Plymouth Rock. So Florida's image has not been as served by its long, complex history as it might have been were Americans a people more aware of the complex stories from our own history. Even the loss of the first war ever for the U.S., failing to conquer the Seminoles is not a topic of ready conversation, even in Florida.

One of the reasons we lose sight of history so easily is doubtless because of the many lightning-fast distractions available to us. But even more important than that, probably, is that we are privileged, or underprivileged, not to have been one of the generations that arrived here first and were thus charged with deciphering Indian geographical place names or coming up with our own for all the new places. When then-recent South Carolina transplants to central Florida named Marion County, the Revolutionary War hero Francis Marion had been dead only forty-nine years, and those new Floridians had scarcely had time to create new heroes of their own, or to know any of the Native Americans or Spanish who had long ago made history there in what became the new home place of the former South Carolinians. When the South Carolinians moved on a few miles farther south and created Sumter County ten years later, the South Carolinian Thomas Sumter had been dead only twenty years. In our own unhistorical time probably no public school student in Sumter County could identify Thomas Sumter, the Gamecock, or Marion, the Swamp Fox, nor could any child in Pensacola likely identify the Spanish general honored in the name of the main thoroughfare, Palafox. If a Jacksonville resident today knows that Jacksonville derives from Andrew Jackson, he is still unlikely to know of William Pope DuVal, whose name is presumably just as important to a knowledge of that place. But he would know the provenance of the name if his father had campaigned for it. Those names have been in use for a long time now, and only the civil rights movement has had sufficient resolve to change many names settled on long ago. So much Florida history is conveyed in the names of remote places, names seldom celebrated. But the decisions of even the most minor local officials would be more studied if it were common among us to know the history conveyed in the place names of Florida.

Being automatically included as a part of the most familiar history conveys on a locale certain privileges. A place associated with the most familiar names in history has a better chance to declare itself off-limits to modern forces of irreversible change. Where a condominium community or nuclear power plant or interstate highway is planned on an utterly unmarked pristine area of Florida marsh, historical preservation is probably more easily accomplished if that marsh goes by a name familiar to everyone for historical significance. If the marsh is known to have been the site of ancient Native

American burials, that place is more apt already to be in public ownership, or the improbability of the acquisition and development of it would be recognizable to the economic forces that might contemplate its development. Public celebration of a place helps create an aura of obligation on the part of the political leadership to find the right combination of historians, conservationists, preservationists, urban planners, publicists, archivists, and writers as well as developers and their construction companies in the unofficial fashioning of the state's official version of the great moments in Florida's long history.

Today's political and economic decisions might more likely be swayed by the number of the electorate who have read a brightly colored pamphlet or seen a brief documentary film, or heard snatches of a popular jingle. If "Way Down Upon the Kissimmee River" were the state song, the Kissimmee would never have been channelized by a Corps of Army Engineers at loose ends, facing budget hearings but still in search of a project to undertake to enhance the serious image of the Corps, but a project just as easily built in a salubrious climate as in the tundra. If the state song were "Way Down Upon the Ocklawaha," there would be no Rodman dam, no remnants of a long-ago proposed cross-Florida barge canal. "Way Down Upon the Crystal River" would have sent Florida Power and Light erecting nuclear cooling towers elsewhere. An astonishing amount of familiarity accrues around the one easy date 1492 and the *Santa Maria*. Florida's history would enjoy a very different status today if Columbus, as the first adelantado, had reached Florida and established St. Augustine. The general public may not know who was the King of England in 1492, or Pope in Rome, and certainly they do not know the names of nations of Native Americans already in Florida in 1492. But had it been Columbus rather than Ponce de León and Pedro Menéndez de Avilés, John D. Rockefeller might have started preservation efforts not in Williamsburg but in St. Augustine, and in the ripple effect that familiar history has on economic development many of the sites of the very earliest human habitation in Florida would be icons of public awareness rather than obliterated beneath parking lots and condominium high-rises.

History is not so much what is known to have occurred but what has been made familiar over the generations at best by the printed page, at worst by imagery arising out of advertising. Among historians today, writing about the earliest European Florida, there is always just a hint of apology, or disappointment that the Europeans who got to Florida first were Spanish, not English, and thus the bearers of the language that ultimately prevailed, as though our Spanish origins made Florida less American, less a player in the grand events of the coming new nation. And that is precisely what has happened. In the most intense national crises Florida has given evidence of unAmerican origins. In the Revolution, Florida remained loyal to King George III. Florida was the last area south of Canada and east of the continental divide to become American. Florida was the last area of the original New World to speak English. It was early to secede, vigorous in the Confederate cause, recalcitrant in forging a new constitution amenable to the Reconstruction-minded Congress after 1865. The first flag of the State of Florida strutted the imperative "Let Us Alone," the exact opposite of the attitude trumpeted by Florida's tourist economy today. That attitude obtained only briefly during the early years of underpopulated and impoverished Florida; since Reconstruction, Florida has been guided more by its lure than by needs.

Florida at times seemed almost innocent amid the political currents during its infancy as a corporate unit, as a colony of a far-distant monarch or within the older, more politically established states it became one of in 1845. Like every other newly-formed state, it has had its moments of human shortcoming. Miscarriages of history, even the most notorious, can achieve a familiarity that serves to ameliorate misdeeds into something that seems less egregious: Harper's Ferry, the Scopes trial, Salem "witches," interning Japanese families, Custer's last stand, instances of the past in a culture and economy moving at warp speed. Even in mellow Florida, there are blots on the scutcheon of "an Indian maiden scattering flowers": Rosewood, the Charley Johns committee, the Groveland Four, channeling the Kissimmee, signing the "Southern Manifesto," phosphate mining, Andrew Sledd's tenure as first president of the University of Florida, seem less consequential in an inviting climate overwhelmed by Disney World, one hundred million tourists, a trillion-dollar economy.

The most direct, confrontational actions resulting in Florida's absorption into the United States are almost wholly the Caesaristic ambitions of Andrew Jackson, a man who had strong emotional ties to the state, but not of pride or affection. Jackson's attitude suggests that Florida's entry into the house of the union was through the back door. Little from those years lends any special aura to anything about Florida's resources or the gifts of its people that attracted American interest other than as a place of refuge for those poor farmers who had been unable to make their fame and fortune in the more settled and organized states of the South. The same pattern would be repeated at the turn of the century, when no one in Florida had the wherewithal to develop a modern Florida and thus left the still almost unoccupied state open to the desires of magnates from elsewhere who did have the wherewithal to develop Florida according to their own designs, regardless of what might have been best for the opening up of the new state. In the last century, when states began campaigns to advertise themselves, Florida proudly called itself "The Everglades State," promoting in simplicity its most notable geographical feature, as though blissfully unaware of fifteen hundred miles of pristine beaches. Later, equally simply, Florida advertised itself as "The Peninsula State." Only after highways and air-conditioning set in motion the frenzy to fill the wild spaces still remaining, did Florida's advertising hook become the more glamorous, fashionable "Sunshine State," featuring bathing beauties galore and sports cars, in the hope of augmenting its lure to the less intrepid traveler.

Florida history would perhaps be very different if the state had been acquired in one of the more glamorous historical incidents, such as Thomas Jefferson's much-admired Louisiana Purchase, or such a crystal clear moment as the battle at the Alamo, or even as a result of the Revolutionary War itself. The acquisition of Florida was not nearly so statesmanlike an accomplishment as Jefferson's acquisition of Louisiana, or so proudly celebrated a nationalistic movement as the Revolution. Florida has been removed generally from the events surrounding the establishing of the United States. It sent no delegate-signers to the Continental Congress, it did not help write the Constitution, it was a Tory haven in the War for Independence, it was not on the path laid down by

Lewis and Clark. No state has been absorbed into the union through such a circuitous, duplicitous route, without benefit of any of the usual processes of deliberative, representative government all of which are so much a part of the way American history is today fondly recalled. Its acquisition was not even the result of open war. In addition to presidential plotting, Florida was regarded as a place where outlaw justice could be accomplished without consequence: Captain Isaac McKeever took Native American organizers Hillis Hadjo and Himollemico under the deception of a British flag rather than their own American flag; Zachary Taylor captured chiefs Blue Snake and Philip, as Joseph Hernandez took Osceola and Con Hadjo, and as Thomas Jesup took an entire tribe, all under the flag of truce; and Andrew Jackson assassinated the British nationals Richard C. Ambrister and Alexander Arbuthnot on the Spanish soil of Florida without benefit of trial. Frederick Dau wrote in 1934 in *Florida Old and New* (New York: G. P. Putnam's Sons), that from 1821 to 1842 Florida "seems to have become one of the greatest liabilities ever assumed by the United States...time and time again the governmental authorities would have welcomed a news item that Florida had some night disappeared and sunk to the bottom of the Atlantic Ocean" (179).

Florida history, then, is not one that is easily called to the attention of the average student of American history. This state was not wrested from a harsh, unforgiving climate, like the barren, wind-swept Great Plains conquered by men and women lovingly called pioneers. Florida did not offer the unyielding terrain of mountains for Lewis and Clark to perform heroics in trailblazing. Its defenders, the Spanish, were not in the prime of their national destiny when circumstances required that they resist the inroads of Americans, who were indeed in the prime of their efforts at nation building. Eighteenth-century Spain was a country whose fantasies of empire were already playing out. Florida must have seemed much like a playground to oncoming Americans even then, except to the soldiers who were sent unwillingly into swamp fastnesses to root out Seminoles fighting for their homes. Florida had not been a participant in any of the rebellious activities, now approvingly recalled, leading up to a war for independence from Europe. Florida must, in fact, have seemed at the time the one area of America most likely to retain its European ties, except that its geography made its Americanization inevitable. It was just too obvious, the peninsula jutting out from the rest of the emerging continent separating Atlantic from Gulf, its location, if not it resources, making it irresistible to the growing new nation. Florida did not come willingly of its own accord into union with the other states, deliberately seeking to confederate with the ever-expanding United States. It was an open territory, devoid after Spanish evacuation of leaders eager to make a state of the union out of it. So it came in time to appeal to sufficient numbers of would-be leaders who had not succeeded in leadership roles elsewhere in the South, and thus acquired the push from within to organize as a state of the union, and subsequently as a state of the Confederacy. But circumstances that now make those early years of becoming a part of the United States inevitable do not suggest an eagerness on the part of Florida, but rather a lack of intensity about becoming American that has been repaid in this century by having been turned into the nation's sandbox, and not the nation's repository of those institutions that have led other states of the union to distinction. What Florida had then is what it still has, if in quantities that have been reduced by lack of proper attention, and they are a history and a natural beauty unique among the treasures brought to the union by its other members.

First published in *Southern Studies: An Interdisciplinary Journal of the South*, X:III-IV (Fall/Winter 2003), 1-10.

5

Florida's Geography

Maps printed in the United States usually show this country
alone, in isolation, without any of the rest of the world included, revealing the United States to be an almost square
country. When we see ourselves on maps of the whole world,
with all the other countries in pink, green, yellow (we are always red or blue), we are the only country very nearly square
anywhere on the globe. It's probably not xenophobia that
makes us want to see ourselves alone so much as it is delight
with the phenomenon of our very nearly square borders, the
only square country anywhere on the planet. Our mapmakers
sensing what will sell, seem to prefer those maps that show
the United States in isolation, exclusive even of its borders
with our two large northern and southern neighbors, the way
countries that are islands may more legitimately do. The
wonder is, that we got to keep our country as square. Politicians being slow to graduate from conquest to the more tedi-

ous task of developing civilizations, the momentum to extend the United States might not have stopped after the Louisiana Purchase, the Mexican War, the Gadsden Purchase, and the Onis Treaty absorbing Florida. But going north beyond the Great Lakes or south beyond the Rio Grande would have cost us the squareness so obvious on the map as it came to be drawn. As the pioneers crossed the Mississippi, they even drew square states, abandoning the earlier fashion of following such natural land formations as mountains or water routes such as rivers and shorelines to define states from one another.

Further expansion, however much one desired, when all that territory of Mexico was on an economic par with the United States, and possessed of an already much older civilization both from its indigenous peoples and from its modern mother, Spain, would have deprived the United States of its coveted, hard-won squareness. Luckily, the physical separation of Alaska and Hawaii spare us the unnecessary explanation and possible embarrassment because they can be disconnected on maps and shown as mere inserts and thus not disturb the symmetry of America's unique squareness. Canada ends in such asymmetrical jaggedness along its top, while Mexico seems to dwindle away toward the south into an unseemliness of ever narrower Spanish-speaking countries, and acquisition of either Mexico or Canada would have compromised American squareness. Canada for all its vast expanse shatters at the edges and doesn't come out square anywhere. Mexico is a backward comma, allowing the U.S. that much more to be square about. Other countries, too, take on shapes that deprive them the squareness the United States so enjoys about itself. Israel is an ancient, primitive dagger. Jordan is a butterfly's profile. India is a human heart, closer to anatomical correctness than the familiar St. Valentine's Day cartoon of the heart. Chile's curvature is indistinguishable from Vietnam's. Italy is a famous boot. England is recognizable, of course, along with Scotland, but only because of a culture that produced so many unwilling, or unwitting, Anglophiles around the world, made up mostly of students from those countries it once ruled. Still, England has no corners. Scotland and Wales give it no help. Neither would all of Ireland. Only the United States has real, actual corners. Three, at least.

The northeast stops where Bangor slides up into place behind the protective barrier of Nova Scotia. San Diego ends the southwest corner abruptly and evenly at Baha California. The northwest corner splinters beyond Seattle into fingerlings indistinguishable between what is American and what is Canadian, but with no large landmark offsetting the square on either side of the border. But one corner of the United States stands out defiantly on its own, denying the U.S. its coveted square perfection, and that is the southeastern one, belonging exclusively to possibly the most recognizable political and geographical outline on earth, an outline much more readily recognizable than that of the entire U.S., an outline anything but square. Florida.

Had Florida been square, a fourth nearly perfect corner would have given the United States total perfection of squareness. If Florida had remained Spanish, as it seemed destined to do for its first three hundred years of European influence, Georgia, preponderantly rectangular north and south, comes closer to a square than Florida, and would have made a nearly perfect fourth corner. Texas is the only other outline that might have made as distinctive a corner, as it possesses much of the requisite squareness. As it is, Florida's lack of squareness is the imperfect resolution to the long outward arc of the east coast of the United States, forming a parabola, dipping in at the last moment of the Georgia coast before bulging once more into the Atlantic to form Cape Canaveral, then tapering gently to its end at Key West. On the west coast of the Florida "corner," far more imaginatively even than the east coast, that grand Gulf arc starts far out into the Caribbean at Mérida on the farther most tip of the Yucatan, sweeping up and over to give coast line to Texas, Louisiana, Mississippi and Alabama before once more sweeping down southward to very nearly complete the Gulf circle, just breaking up into the keys before dwindling out at Key West, its ultimate period at Tortuga. What is known today as the Gulf of Mexico might just as easily, almost does, in fact, make instead a giant inland lake. It would be so prominent it would have been called a sea, illustrious as the Caspian, the Aral, or the Black, to say nothing of the Mediterranean. The Sea of Mexico would have been to the New World as the Mediterranean is to the old, the midway point of the continents. The coastline of the Gulf of Mexico is the most elaborate gesture in all of the earth's often dramatic littoral geography. But there it is. As wholly unsquare as it so obviously is, Florida is the undisputed corner, the most recognizable, obvious corner to any land mass anywhere, one of John Donne's "round earth's imagined corners," sticking out into the midst of the three seas as it does.

Peninsula Florida's geographical distinctiveness proved irresistible to Europeans five hundred years ago, a natural landing site for westward-leading sailing ships. It still proves irresistible, the world's only perfectly realized, and exploited, combination of geography and climate and development. Heartland Americans tired of endless cornfields head to Florida today as ineluctably as Spaniards did across the stormy Atlantic half a millennium ago, as they have begun in recent decades to head in ever increasing hordes to an absolutely square Colorado because it rises above the map as unimaginably peaked as altogether flat Florida offers littoral curves. Maybe it is as simply explained as the obviousness of it. If Florida decanted upward to a volcano in the middle of the Everglades, the whole northward-looking state depending away from it, getting there, all the way to the end, might not be so obvious as to be appealing, even compelling. But that isn't the case. Over land it's an easy downhill slide all the way down Florida, drawing ever closer to dead-even level with the sea's edge. The Altamaha river valley across middle Georgia marks the fall line, the last remotely hilly terrain before the landscape flattens out and rushes on into Florida. At sea, for the Europeans on sailing ships five hundred years ago, there was no uphill climb over any kind of land barrier once afloat out in tiny wooden boats on the high seas. The trip to Florida is even easier now. If Florida had ended up as a series of rocky crags along the east coast, balancing out the Rocky Mountains to the west, the peninsula would have offered its own resistance. The allure would have had to wait for the twentieth century and the automobile and the highways subsidized by a government willing to put mobility for everyman in the same category Ferdinand and Isabella put mobility for the stalwart Columbus. Ponce de León's has become commonplace, shared now not by the intrepid few but by one hundred million geographically unchallenged tourists per annum. No wonder Florida is not the easiest place in the world to find any sense of the reality usually afforded by terra firma, a natural expression of the graceful mix there of equal parts land and water.

In the long-ago age of exploration and discovery, of even so delightful a place to be first to visit as Florida, the rivers didn't cooperate. The rivers of Florida, with one exception, keep themselves largely to Florida. Unlike the great rivers of America, the rivers of Florida do not connect numerous river port cities along a meandering course across half a dozen states. Only the Apalachicola could carry early travelers inland any distance beyond Florida itself. But even at its longest reach, to Atlanta, the Apalachicola, which becomes the Chattahoochee just fifty miles across Florida from the sea, is largely un-navigable. The Perdido and Choctawhatchee begin tenuously, haltingly, in Alabama, and the Ochlocknee and Suwanee rise faintly in Georgia, but none of these allow more than canoe access until well into Florida. Otherwise, the rivers of Florida do not mingle with the waters of bordering states. They carry no one downstream from elsewhere into Florida. They never allowed for the development of commercial intercourse among diverse ports elsewhere in the South. Thomas Jefferson sent Lewis and Clark up the Missouri to the west on a river road across most of the United States through some of its most impenetrable terrain. But he couldn't have sent them to chart Spanish Florida on its rivers. No river goes the length of Florida. But the Spaniards and early American invaders didn't need a river. The land itself offered no barriers beyond vast swamps, and they are never too deep to traverse, at least not to the adventurer willing to brave the prickly vegetation that mats such a lush setting. The earliest European visitors could just walk right in. And they did, led by Ponce de León, followed by de Narváez, de Soto, de Avilés, and others, their discoveries followed up by the more thorough exploration of an Englishman, Puc Puggy, as the Timucua would call William Bartram.

The lure of a geography called by so melodious a name as "Florida" has always been more possessive than it might have been had it been called by a more pedestrian, or predictable name. The custom then was to name new places after the saint's day of their discovery. So Florida might have become Easter Island, St. Eostre. Under other circumstances of the long-ago day Ponce de León would have landed on some other day than Easter, the holiest of days in the Christian year. But any other day would have been the feast day of one or another of the saints of the Catholic year. And Ponce de León would have honored that saint with a name that might have lasted as long as the name of the flowery day of the Easter feast has beckoned folks to the peninsula. Instead of just a city in St. Augustine's honor, the whole state might have become Augustiniana. Or Ponce de León might have honored the Spanish patron, so the name given the beautiful, simple geography might have been Iagoiola, alongside the Island of Hispaniola. In any case, Ponce de León and the Spaniards dwelled with the immortals in mind, unlike the English, who honored their earthly heroes, gave us George's Georgia, Charles' Carolina, Elizabeth the Virgin's Virginia, or even the New Hampshire's-York's-England's. Had Ponce de León come ashore to dwell with the natives long enough to have a Spanish equivalent for their names, as the Pilgrims at Plymouth did with Massachusetts, as well as the Southerners who got Mississippi out of Meschacebe, or Tennessee out of the Tenasi, Alabamians from the Alibamu, we might have a geography called Timucuana, or Tequestiana, Calusaland or Jororoland. We might even have kept the beautiful place name Apalachia to ourselves, descriptive only of our peninsular geography, instead of having it turned over to inland mountains by erroneous early mapmakers, who thought those mountains started at the Gulf sea, where the Indians of that name dwelled. Luckily, an early generation absorbed the English pronunciation of those old Indian tribes and held faithfully to them, well ahead of the generation that came to fear and hate, then murder the natives of America. Surely only ignorance of the Indian source of names preserved those names. The Spanish had actually started at Pensacola on the east coast before the beginning of St. Augustine. They might have done worse than naming the new place for the western aborigines, the Apalachee. As it is, we do indeed still have the small town beside the beautiful river, both going by the musical name of Apalachicola. But Ponce de León arrived first, automatically taking all the naming rights, and he arrived not on a mere saint's day but on the holiest day of his Christian year. There must be a destiny that shapes our ends, after all, to immortalize the holiest of days in the sweetest of all names, a brief, easy application of the name for the Feast of Flowers, Pascua Florida.

Leif Erickson might have had the privilege of naming this peninsula geography, adding a Nova Norway to the overlays of New England, Nouvelle France, as well as Nueva España. There are no flowers blooming there in the frozen north early enough to celebrate Woden, or Thor, who have had days of the week named after them in recompense for losing the wonder of geographical place names to the Spaniards, possessors of a far more musical language. No other simple fact of its geography defines the beauty of Florida more memorably than its musically Hispanic name. As the English from Hampshire and Jersey simply offered reminiscence of home place in the old world, Ponce de León might have been egoist enough to honor both his home place and himself and call this new old place New Leonia. As a good Catholic he might have acted similarly to the French Catholics in Louisiana who honored their early heroes, or even have designated us a Philippines seven years before Magellan's voyage in honor of the same Philip II Ponce de León, too, served. Ponce de León might justifiably have named Florida as predictably as the English Catholics who, in the raging fashion of Maryology of that day, called their new world Mary's Land. The Spanish would at least have offered the greater musicality of a Marialand.

Though it makes up in its own inimitable way one of the corners of the lower forty-eight states, Florida is not the end of anything, no boxed-in corner. It is more like a beginning. Though the oldest of places in this country, it feels to so many who are attracted to it in this mobile era more like a very new place, a place of beginnings, not endings, even to those who come in retirement, late in life. Florida looks as though the gods of winds and seas and glaciers creating its curvatures meant to go on to create another whole continent shaped, probably, something like South America. But on the whole, when the glacier melted somewhat and they got a good look at what they had thus far, those gods were obviously quite pleased with what they had done, and so left off with a satisfying sigh sloughing out into the keys, a final dot of punctuation with Dry Tortugas. Kansans or Nebraskans, Arizonans or New Mexicans coming out of those endless stretches of dry hot plains devoid of great expanses of water, must wonder, coming into Florida, at the mingling here of water and sky. Anyone from a dry climate who has dipped into the frigid crystal of a Florida underground-fed spring must know that the gods felt no need to make another whole continent here or anywhere, with such delights, already at hand. If, however, the aridity back home means very little humidity, the air one comes up into out of a cool dip in a Florida spring will offer less comfort than the Kansan might have bargained for. Florida has all it can do already, without worrying about humidity, its geography disallowing the United States its fourth more or less exactly square corner, thus denying this square country at least one of the edges that would have allowed this country a squareness unequalled anywhere else on earth.

2014

6

Post-bellum Florida: Southerly, but Not Southern

Florida has not struck many non-Floridians as much of a part of a South that includes certifiably Southern places such as Alabama, Mississippi, or South Carolina. During the brief years of the Confederate States of America, Florida did its part to fit in with the rest of the South. But Abraham Lincoln was not convinced. Florida was less committed to the Confederacy than any other state besides Arkansas. So, Lincoln commissioned his twenty-five year old secretary, John Hay, a major, and sent him to Jacksonville to get signatures on enough loyalty oaths to secure Florida's three electoral votes, and a seat in Congress for Hay. But Hay failed to get the ten percent of Floridians to sign oaths for his congressional seat, and the troops protecting him lost the battle of Olustee. But the war was nearly over anyway. Since Lincoln's day, countless other observers mesmerized by beach sand or a booming economy have found too little cotton here, or whatever else they might have been looking for, to describe Florida as Southern. From the standpoint of the whole story of the South itself, aside from the short life of the actual Confederacy, Florida has found, at best, an ill fit in this region.

However unlike the rest of the South it seems today, Florida's identity with the South was clearer to some than to others. Not yet known worldwide as a playground, and far removed still from having become a mega-sized state among the union, Florida was, at one point, more nearly recognizably Southern. In the 1911 edition of the *Encyclopaedia Britannica*, the most literary issue of that famous compendium, the remarks on Florida are straightforward enough: "Florida is the most southern state..." This framework of reference though referred to its geographical location, not cultural or spiritual backgrounds—the source of Southern identity. No particular mindset seems implied by the British writer within the section of the encyclopaedia called "Florida." Yet, the state that the writer in that edition of the encyclopaedia goes on to describe is in no way set apart from its Southern neighbors.

Florida's membership, in good standing in the romance and ruin of the old Confederacy, steadily eroded in the twentieth century as the one that counted most for what is special as "southern." Most of the South has, since its inception, been English, which disenfranchised Florida in much of the discussion of the history of the South. Hegemonic English asserts itself early in the writing of Southern history: "Although in possession of English America for many hundreds or thousands of years, the Indian had made little or no modification of his environment," writes A. E. Parkins in *The*

South: Its Economic-Geographical Development in 1938. Parkins omitted Florida because it had only been ruled by England for twenty years. A further sampling of written opinion extends the concept of the South as including only those parts English in origin. I. A. Newby, a more nearly contemporary historian of the South, wrote *The South: A History* in 1978. After opening with a chapter called "The Search for a Central Theme," Newby goes to the beginning of the South's history with a chapter called "The Developing South Since 1607," thus ignoring European, albeit Spanish, Florida beginning in 1513. Even the historians of Florida acknowledge the absence of Florida in the national and regional discussions of history. "A very prevalent opinion, frequently expressed both in conversation and in print, but nevertheless without foundation," Frederick W. Dau writes in *Florida: Old and New* in 1934, "is that from 1512 to 1762, we have no authentic Florida history," thus moving the origins of Florida right up to the point of British possession. The Southern historian Thomas D. Clark writes in *The Emerging South* in 1968 of the growing revenues from tourism, especially in Florida, and offers that condescending aside, "It may be true that in the long run Southern history and atmosphere in the raw will be a more profitable and dependable source of income to the region than cotton ever was, even in its golden era." Another historian, Neal R. Pearce, was not willing to begin Florida's Southern chapter even as early as the date of absorption into an English-speaking union. He writes in *The Deep South States of America* in 1972, "the real history of Florida awaited the 1880s and the arrival of the first big promoters." Moreover, "the state as a whole has broken so sharply from its region that most of its ties to the Deep South today are an accident of geography." Florida would likely have been no less embraced by historians of Southern self-consciousness had it become a breeding ground of abolitionism. Florida's inclusion in what is American rather than Spanish would have been helped if Florida, divided into two parts, East and West Florida, separated by the Suwanee, had ever been looked upon as the fourteenth and fifteenth colonies, as they might well have been, if not indeed, as the first and second original colonies, older by a century than Plymouth or Jamestown.

Even the less rigidly academic, presumably "softer" discipline of social science gives Florida credit for little of the rebelliousness that might have led to Civil War, a prerequisite attitude to being considered a part of the South. The first of the seminal accounts of the social South is the almost biblically proportioned text of Southern studies, Ulrich B. Phillips' *Life and Labor in the Old South* in 1929. Phillips notes that at the time of the purchase of Florida by the United States, "East Florida was reckoned at fifteen thousand and of West Florida at five thousand, all described alike as loiterers." Phillips writes Florida out of the South in this first of the great Southern social studies texts: "Florida formed in the main a southward extreme of the United States rather than an integral part of the South." The next of the now-famous Southern social studies, V. 0. Key's *Southern Politics,* declared in 1949 that "Florida is unlike other states of the South in many ways and, in truth, it is scarcely a part of the South." Though "it occasionally gives a faintly tropical rebel yell, it is a world of its own." When social science gave way to more popular treatments by journalists, Florida looked even less like a legitimate part of the South. In *A Southerner Discovers the South* in 1938, Jonathan Daniels comes upon "one whole lake near

Cross City in amazing and beautiful bloom -- and all wasted on native Floridians." Farther south, "'This is such a barren' I said to myself, 'that nothing would grow on it but a millionaire.'" Finally, "I knew I was out of the South and I turned north in Yankee Florida to get back to it."

With the perspective of a few facts from those fateful war years, however, Florida's Southerness seems less arguable, despite how little Florida's tourist economy has come to look like the rest of the South. Florida was sufficiently ready to rebel that it was the third of eleven states to secede, beating out even Virginia, the mother of the Confederacy itself. Florida took but a mere single day longer to secede than the quintessentially rebellious and non-conforming Mississippi, the most Southern of states. Florida's secessionist convention must have been in the mood to secede, despite the efforts of moderate former Territorial Governor Richard Keith Call. In the old Florida towns along the northern border like Quincy, Marianna, and Madison, companies of soldiers began to form at once. Before the war had been lost, Florida sent more soldiers per capita to the cause than any other Southern state. So Florida showed no reluctance during the origins of the Southern mystique to be a part of it.

What would seem to be an element of Florida's image as a Southern state is the fate of Tallahassee. Southerners take state capitals seriously. The choice of a capital city is less likely to be a common-sense location, like the geographical midcenter of the state, as it would be it in the midwest. The more likely choice would be a city that seemed best suited by reason of charm in the sense that a real estate agent would understand. It is a decision in which Southerners take pride. Florida's capital city was a star city of the South, the only

Southern capital never to fall into Yankee hands as the result of siege, even though the rest of the state had been captured. Milledgeville, Nashville, Columbia, Montgomery, Jackson, Baton Rouge, Raleigh and, of course, Richmond fell to Union troops. Few of the battles of the Civil War were fought in Florida, but a crucial one for Florida was the Battle of Natural Bridge, waged to capture Tallahassee. Only a month before defeat came at Appomattox, long after Florida and the South were exhausted by the war, a ragged band of young boys and very old men held the Union army at bay, and gave Florida's capital the signal distinction of being the only state capital not to fall. Federal troops did not enter Tallahassee until May 10, 1865, when General Edward McCook arrived to assume military command of Florida, a full month after Lee's surrender. Tallahassee's small moment in history might have been expected to serve Florida better in securing and holding, even in this century of indifference to history, credentials as a Southern place, especially since Southerners usually exhibit more interest in regional history than most other locations in the country.

Yet, an irony of history is that defeat became the basis of Southern identity, so that Tallahassee, by having remained uncaptured, lost some of the romance it would have had if it been captured in a protracted siege like Richmond or Columbia, battles that have become legendary in the story of the Confederacy. It is less than certain, though, that Florida's uncaptured capital would have offered an image that would have preserved the spirit of Southern intransigence for the state. In a century in which regional consciousness and pride of place have largely given way to mobility, the South is the one region to maintain a sense of provincial separate-ness.

What is questionable, even with the evidence of the map of the United States for corroboration, is whether Florida has a place in the constellation of Southern states. Far from having sought hegemony, one might wonder today if Florida has even a modest niche in the amphictyony of Southern states. The closing years of the war, like the opening years, offer evidence that Florida did not acquire its reputation as less Southern than any other member of the Confederacy until later. The man who led Florida as Governor throughout the entire duration of the war, except for the last eight days of the life of General Lee's army, was John Milton, a direct descendant of the fabled John Milton of *Paradise Lost*. An antebellum South, under the spell of Robert Burns and Walter Scott, probably recognized the significance of the lineage involved in Florida's wartime leadership even if pride in the significance of his literary forebears has slipped away from us in this unliterary era. Governor John Milton felt so keenly the burden of Florida's Southern history that he took his own life a week before Appomattox, the South's demise being clear to him. Surely, such sacrifice vouchsafes credentials sufficient to provide at least some preserving patina of amber to Florida's Southern identity.

Florida exhibited leadership deliberately and consciously Southern to make its diminished Southern appearance in modern times a less than predictable phenomenon. The aggressive pace at which Florida rushed to secede did not imply in 1861 the intention to go to war as much as Florida's desire to find its rightful place in the Confederacy. Still undeveloped in that era, Florida could hardly have rattled a sabre savagely enough to suggest that it sought hegemony even in the seceding South. Admitted to the Union such a brief time before secession—only fifteen years, and the administrations of only three governors—Florida had little time to shape itself into a state preparing for war, when compared to long-established states. Four Southern states were prominent colonies in the establishment of the larger republic. They had three full generations in which to get ready to go their own way. A fifth seceding state, Tennessee, though not an original colony, barely missed out, entering into statehood in 1796. Alabama, Florida's neighbor, was organized as a state for only a generation when war demanded the equal participation of the eleven states. Florida, also in its infancy, did its part for the Confederacy as chief supplier of beef and salt, which during this time was as vital as powder and shot.

More importantly, Florida offers proof of a political mettle not exhibited since the defeat, having supplied the Confederacy with the only member of the presidential cabinet to remain at Jefferson Davis' side throughout the entire duration of the war. Stephen Mallory was the only Confederate cabinet member to serve co-terminus with the life of the country he served. Had the proposal to colonize the state with all the South's freed slaves passed, Florida would have remained to this day the most visible reminder of the war.

Florida's devotion to the South did not end as the war ended at Appomattox. One hundred years ago, Tampans rioted in the streets in protest of American soldiers enroute to Cuba, who de-trained there wearing blue uniforms, more than thirty years after the defeat of Florida's troops in gray. It was Florida's intention throughout the nineteenth century to remain as Southern as its sister states. Lt. Col. Flint, commander at Tallahassee who reported to General Pope in Atlanta, wrote in 1866 that "the only report received since the 15th (from Cedar Keys) expresses the belief that the people in that vicinity may be as disloyal to the government as they were three years ago. This maybe, and probably is true of a considerable class of the community not only in Cedar Keys but throughout the state" (W. W. Davis, *The Civil War and Reconstruction in Florida*. Vol. LIII, Studies in History, Economics, and Public Law. New York: Columbia University Press, 1913, p. 443).

Nevertheless, Florida's Southern credentials are today very much in dispute, although less throughout the rest of the country than among Southerners, because of its present appearance of being populated only by transients and developers. Non-Southerners can still recognize remnants of lingering rebelliousness amid the beach clutter better than many Southerners can, although the rest of the nation does not find Florida's lingering Southerness offensive enough to make them shun the sunshine state. But for the lack of passion for history among those flocking to the beach, or among those waiting at countless beach shops and motels to serve them, Florida's Southern ties cannot be entirely dismissed. As all politics is local, all history is provincial. The South's identity, as well as the national destiny, is inextricably tied to that conflict. Despite the cumulative effect of the five hundred years of the European civilization that have prevailed in the New World, the Civil War is still the single most defining moment in American history. There were only two sides. To imagine Florida as a non-participant, or as a participant on any but the losing side of the most important signal event in American history, is to discredit a relevant part of the past. Only now does the beach appear to be neutral territory, where vacationers come in order to forget the conflicts and tensions of real life. Florida was there, alongside those states whose regional identities are not in question, even a century and a half beyond the conflict. The tourist economy in Florida probably would not rise significantly from an enhancement of the state's regional character. But the state's inability to remain in the sisterhood of Southern states bears some resemblance to the state's failure to have any image at all except as the great national sandbox.

It cannot be merely the beaches, however, that deny Florida a place in Southern consciousness. Every state in the old Confederacy, except Tennessee and Arkansas, have beaches. If we were a people particularly conscious of history, Florida's failure to retain its identity as a Southern state might be owing to lingering resentment connected to coastal defenses in the South in 1861. Coastal defenses were vital to the cotton trade abroad not only to the economy of the South, but to Confederate foreign policy. Of these Southern defenses, only three remained out of Confederate control the entire war, and all three were forts on Florida beaches—Fort Pickens on Santa Rosa Island, Fort Taylor at Key West, and Fort Jefferson on Dry Tortugas. These sites never became battle grounds because they were never surrendered by Union garrisons to be commandeered by Confederates. But an unfallen capital like Tallahassee, a governor who faced death rather than Florida's defeat, plus all the salt and beef consumed by Confederate troops, should offer some compensating balance.

Travel conditions in the nineteenth century may have meant that as a result of its geographical location, Florida was never truly admitted to sisterhood among the Southern states. Its outsider status was apparent even during the war. No

Florida city was important enough for William Sherman to capture and offer to Abraham Lincoln as a Christmas gift, as he did Savannah, Georgia. No less, this slight comes not from the most hated of enemy generals, but from the highest Southern leader, President Davis himself. Of the ten states of the Confederacy east of the Mississippi, Florida was the only one never to receive a rallying visit by the president. That hypothetical presidential visit might amount these days to no more than a rusting, kudzu-shrouded historical marker on some long-abandoned railroad siding, but the opportunity, whatever it might have been worth to Florida's image as a Southern state, was lost.

More than a Confederate president has ignored Florida. Though Truman, Kennedy, and Nixon enjoyed the sunshine, Florida never became a regular whistle stop on their journeys. The first six presidents of the United States never saw Florida, and the seventh, Andrew Jackson, had so little taste for the place that he never came back as president after conquering and governing it.

Southern history is a complicated study, but Confederate history is simpler. It was only one presidential term long, only one war to fight, no treaty by the name of some foreign city far removed from the war, only one president, no reelection campaign, and no vice president succeeding an assassinated president. There was none of the murky quagmire of ongoing foreign and domestic policies complicating the chronology of that other federal enterprise, the one headquartered not on the James, but on the Potomac. The South had only one election, one president, one term, one administration, one war, which led to a simpler and less complicated chronology than virtually any other sovereignty in the history of the world. A visit to Florida by President Davis might have drawn it more securely into that brief historical drama that has been long-lived mostly as a romance. But Florida has not found itself at home in the tightly woven fabric of the South. Only the St. Augustine birthplace of Confederate General E. Kirby Smith once prevented Florida's total discredit by CSA enthusiasts, and now that is gone. If Andrew Jackson had been born in Florida, rather than merely conquering it or becoming its first American governor, Florida's relationship to the South would today probably be quite different. Yet, he is perhaps the very progenitor of today's transient Floridian. What he wrought here could hardly be reduced to vacation exercises, yet as conqueror in two long wars and territorial governor for a term of three years, he nevertheless managed to spend only a mere two hundred four days total in Florida, a percentage equivalent to the modern-day "snowbird."

Being "born there" is an essential part of the Southern code. Native is a concept the South understands well enough to turn into standard operating procedure. In the early years of Florida there could not easily have been many individuals, if any, who might have gone from being born there to being governor. But among all the governors from 1821 to 1873, when the governorship went to the first native Floridian, almost all were native Southerners. From 1821 until 1872, Florida governors were natives of North Carolina (Andrew Jackson, his friend John Henry Eaton, and William Dunn Moseley), Virginia (William Pope DuVal, Richard Keith Call, and Thomas Brown), South Carolina (Robert Raymond Reid, James E. Broome, and Madison Starke Perry), Georgia (John Milton and Abram K. Allison), Fairfield, New York (William Marvin, but only through the dubious offices of Reconstruction), Russellville, Kentucky (David Shelby Walker), and Littleton, Massachusetts (Harrison Reed). Notwithstanding the two Yankees, the list of six Carolinians, three Virginians, two Georgians, and one Kentuckian should suggest a mingling of interconfederate affairs sufficient to include Florida retrospectively in at least a modest role in the Cotton Kingdom. It was not until after 1873 that election brought the first native Floridian to office, fifty years into its American period.

With such good Southern connections, Florida Southerners wonder what it takes for the state to be considered Southern. The symbol with the most immediate, impassioned response is the famous battle flag. The bars of the sometimes infamous "stars and bars" is not an accidental crossing of two red stripes that provide a space to display the stars representing the seceding states, but a cross drawn from ancient usage. The cross of Saint Andrews, familiar by its place at the center of flags from the Union Jack to the most famous of Confederate battle flags, appears prominently, still in red on a field of white, as the official flag of Florida. It also reappears on the flags of Georgia, until recently, and Mississippi, in a manner that deliberately reminiscences the Confederacy. This is not necessarily true of Alabama and Florida's appropriation of the red cross flag, which is identical except for the seal at the crossing on Florida's version. That red cross of St. Andrew, so prominently spread across the entire length and breadth of its flag, gives Florida a connection that goes far beyond the era of the Civil War itself. It is the same pattern as the Cross of Burgundy of Philip II under whose aegis St. Augustine was originally settled three hundred fifty years before the South adopted the cross of St. Andrew to distinguish the Confederacy from the Union's horizontal stripes.

The flags of Burgundy and the Confederacy aside, how-ever, St. Andrew's cross is further identified with the South through the Scottish half of the Scotch-Irish, the South's orig-inal white Anglo-Saxon yeomanry, who settled in the moun-tainous backbone of the South known as Appalachia. Appala-chia seems at first glance enough miles away in itself to disen-franchise Florida, so obviously removed from the glorious mountains of the South. But "Appalachia," that most appeal-ing and ubiquitous of Southern sobriquets after "Dixie" itself, is not a Scotch or Irish name, and is not indigenous to the mountains themselves or to anyone aboriginal to that area. The name "Appalachia" is in fact borrowed directly from Florida, derived from the Apalachee Indians of North Flori-da, all of whom were dying off from disease and deprivation just as the Scotch-Irish immigrants were arriving to settle into mountain coves. Early map makers had heard, and subse-quently recorded, that the Apalachee Indian territory extend-ed all the way from the Florida coast up to the mountains, four hundred miles north of the region of the Florida Indians known as Apalachees. Geography can be as uncertain as guarantees of honest Southerness. Exactitude about the Ap-palachians remains somewhat elusive still today. *Webster's Col-legiate* asserts that those famous mountains begin in Pennsyl-vania and proceed southward; Random House, on the contra-ry, believes that the same mountains begin in Alabama and proceed northward. Though the irony persists through the magic of geographical place names that the South's most dis-tinctive region after antebellum splendors received its name from Florida, this has done little to endear Florida to profes-sional Southerners and their provincial views of what consti-tutes the South.

What it takes to be Southern, at least in the minds of those who keep the accounts on such matters, is something not to be found in Florida. Though Southern in proximity and the last slave state created by the United States Congress before refusing to allow further extension of slavery, Florida is not of the South. This is a coveted category for such places as Nashville, Charlottesville, Baton Rouge or Savannah, the kinds of places where the outlines of Southerness are customarily authorized. Of all the Southern states, plus twenty-five non-Southern states, Florida is the only one not to contribute one drop to the tributaries of the otherwise all-encompassing Mississippi River, placing it in a category with such states as Maine and Oregon. Florida, then, is as much in geographical and spiritual isolation as it actually appears to one looking down at it on the globe. It protrudes out from all the rest as if trying to slide away from association, a state in withdrawal. The contours of most of the states of the South suggest more of a sense of connectedness, in contrast to Florida's shying away. The average Southern state shares borders with at least four other states, allowing for a good bit of acculturation across borders. Tennessee has borders with eight other states, making it the most connected. Kentucky, on the other hand, also has eight borders, but suffers the schism of four Southern borders and four borders with Yankee states to the north. Florida connects with only two states, half the average number. While some states are made more Southern by their neighbors, especially if a place like Mississippi happens to be the neighbor, Florida's geography suggests a pulling away from common borders. It becomes less and less Southern as the peninsula sharpens to the south, away from Georgia or Alabama, and moves closer to the distinctly Latin/Caribbean sights and sounds that do not bring to mind the slightest ghostly reminder of the old Confederacy. One instinctively wonders if Florida would fail so completely to pass muster with Southerners if Mississippi, rather than the Gulf of Mexico, formed its western border; Alabama, instead of the Atlantic, its eastern. Might Florida be more appreciated for its Southern heritage if the St. Johns flowed all the way north to join a tributary of the Mississippi? Would Florida seem more Southern if the gracefully squared dome of the old capital in Tallahassee were pockmarked with Yankee cannonballs, as South Carolina's is, rather than serving to remind onlookers that it never succumbed to invading Union troops? Or are beaches just too unlike the Delta, too unlike Black Belt cotton plantations, or too crowded with accents far removed from the Southern drawl?

Florida's rivers do not run to the Mississippi. Florida has no mountains. Even more painful is the theft of Florida's aborigines' Appalachian name, for a geographical feature which is almost a tantamount prerequisite among Southern states. But the absence of characteristics inherently necessary have not deprived other states of their Southern-hood. Louisiana has no mountains, but it has the Mississippi River, easily exempting it from the mountain prerequisite. Mississippi itself has no mountains, but it has not only the Mississippi River but also the Delta, hardly less questionable a Southern entity than the river itself. Other than those two exempted states, the rest of the South virtually ranked for its degree of Southern belonging by the height of its peaks. The dean of literary critics has written that Southern literature is a piedmont, not coastal invention. This is despite the fact that the South began at the coastline and remained so until the younger sons of a second generation grew restless under primogeniture and moved, in desperation, to the less promising agrarian possibilities in the mountains. The dean's delineation of Southern literature helps explain why so few Florida writers account for many pages of coverage in the celebrated *History of Southern Literature*. Among Southern states, North Carolina is highest, followed by Tennessee, Virginia, Georgia, South Carolina, and Alabama. This is almost the exact order of precedence in which the critics of Southern literature would line up the states for literary honors. The lowest, Alabama, comes in at a mere 2,405 feet above sea level, leaving Florida completely out of the picture. Florida seems to almost sink, in fact, into the sea's horizon around the entire perimeter of the state. Florida is virtually at sea level, rising a mere 345 feet out of the water only once at its very highest point. This highest point in Florida is nearly in Alabama, and a full seven hundred miles north of Miami.

It is hardly surprising that Florida's Southern characteristics resist definition. It has not been much easier to define what Southern is, even at its most recognizable. To be authentically Southern, a place has to have that certain feel of being old in a peculiarly Southern way. Feeling "New South" never counts. Atlanta is regarded by many associations of academic, professional, and business people as a good non-Southern place to convene without going to the expense of leaving the South, preventing what would thus amount to a contribution of Southern dollars to a Yankee economy. Charlotte and Birmingham have a similar image problem, while places such as Nashville, Charleston, Richmond or Mobile appeal as authentically Southern. But Florida, the oldest of places, does not feel old in the Southern manner, except in a few small towns across north Florida that are close enough to Georgia or Alabama to take on airs from more reliably Southern locales. In most instances, the great modern cities of Florida are not its most ancient cities, as might be expected. St. Augustine and Pensacola, Florida's ancients, cannot hold out against Miami or Orlando. Even the most Southern of north Florida's towns have lost their old Southern look to the modern look that results from widening highways or shopping malls gutting old downtown areas that once had courthouse squares at the center. The institution most rigorously anti-Southern in its treatment of charmingly unique architecture, the local school board, razes once-beautiful older city and town schools for newer, consolidated schools on the outskirts of town, surrounded by disfiguring parking lots. Post offices and public libraries, once among local jewels of brickwork, suffer the same ignominy. In this South, Florida paces way ahead of the Old South, although behind in educational policies designed to instill into oncoming generations the best sense of regional pride.

One identifying Southern characteristic that might be claimed by Florida's Indians, if not Florida's governing majority, is rebelliousness. Florida's Indians, the Seminoles, though dispatched before the Civil War, take their name from a word meaning "separateness," or "dissenters." Though the definition of the name "Seminole" is not universally agreed on, most dictionaries show the name deriving from the American Spanish "cimarron." But the *American Heritage Dictionary* in particular connects the French "maron," or fugitive slave, to "cimarron" as a definition for the verb form "to be marooned," wistfully suggestive of the Seminoles having been marooned from their original Appalachian homes. In the most intense national crises, Florida has given evidence of the same spirit of rebellious separateness. In the American Revolution, Floridians remained loyal to King George III, providing a haven to fleeing Tories. Florida was the last area of the New America to speak English. Florida was early to secede, vigorous in the pursuit of the Confederate Cause, and reluctant, even to the point of truculence, to forge a constitution amenable to the Reconstructionist Congress after 1865.

It has not been modernity that has muted Florida's Southerness, however, as much as a reputation for a certain kind of moderation. The worse the reputation for recalcitrance of a Southern state, the more certifiably Southern it seems to become. The more progressive, the more enlightened, the less belligerent, the less resistant to change, the harder it seems to be for a state to lay claim to the southernmost elements of its rightful heritage. The notoriety of the South's most savage slavetrader is captured in Harriet Beecher Stowe's Simon Legree, while Florida's most famous slavetrader, Zephaniah Kingsley, is less well known for his use of the whip than his use of the pen in writing tracts promoting decent treatment of blacks. Atlanta and Miami contest to be the capital of that new, more moderate South, inspired by Florida's example, as Montgomery and Richmond contested once for the leadership of the Old South.

What is Southern at its best is an exaggeration of effect, or of image. Compared to a reputation for enormity of experience elsewhere in the South, Florida seems bland. Throughout the South, beyond Florida, cotton fields were always bigger and plantations grander; more to the point of the Southerness of a place. Race riots were fiercer, prisons more dreaded, iced tea sweeter, college football rivalries fiercer, drawls thicker, rivers longer, deeper, swifter. Elsewhere in the South, images are sharper and clearer as though the events that led to them were more important to the people there. In Florida, on the other hand, life perhaps seemed easier because there was always a vacation atmosphere beneath so much balmy sunshine, thus leading to less exacerbated, less sharply defining moments. Tennessee is famous for the acrimony of its Scopes Trial, the literary prowess of the Fugitive-Agrarians, and the frontier valor of Daniel Boone, while the trials of Ruby Lee McCollum and Clarence Earl Gideon in Florida never seemed as sensational. A trial removed Alcee Hastings from one office only to make possible his election to a higher one. Hernando de Soto's adventures, which began in Florida and far riskier than Daniel Boone's, seem foreign, peculiar, eccentric to the point of foolish, and never tie in to Florida's beginnings as Southern.

A quality of pastel pervades Florida, making it somehow different, unlike places and events regularly Southern. The Spanish-French heritage that is quaint in New Orleans is derisively foreign in Florida. Gary Cooper made Tennessee's Sergeant York famous; and Captain Richard Bradford, the first Florida officer to fall in the Civil War, is memorialized in the name of an entire county. But Bradford never equaled the legend of the Tennessee sergeant, or the fabulous events at the Alamo nearly a century earlier. Alabama, famous for the ferocity of the Scottsboro Boys, is even more well-known for the invasion of the boll weevil. This boll weevil invasion is more famous and more storied in Southern lore than Florida's fight with the equally destructive hordes of fruit flies. "Boll Weevil" sounds like a term relative exclusively to the Southern lexicon, like "y'all," while Florida's menace is identified by its non-Southern non-Anglo-Saxon adjective "Mediterranean." Louisiana's Mardi Gras and quadroon balls, South Carolina's mesmerizing Charleston gardens, Georgia's Leo Frank lynching and Margaret Mitchell's novel, virtually every hamlet of Virginia bearing Civil War scars, all seem Southern. But nothing in Florida equals the intensity or is eccentric or outrageous enough to be certifiably Southern.

Among the most defining characteristics of Southerners is separateness, or isolation from the rest of America. Southern states did not come together easily in confederation, each wanting to win the war on its own, to see itself as a sovereign state. Today, with only memories of that war to pull them toward each other, the Southern states now see themselves as a unit, but a unit still separate from the rest of the states. Florida seems beyond even that, despite the appearance of separation so implicit in its geography. Separateness is a part of Florida even in its Indian heritage. The demise of the aboriginal tribes in Florida was not a pattern repeated in all American Indian cultures, nor did it mean the end of an Indian presence in Florida. The place of the Calusas, Timucuans, Apalachees, Aiis, Jeagas and Miamis was taken by runaway Creeks who became the Seminoles—the isolates. Whatever may be discovered linguistically about the history of their name, they were, from the beginning, separated from the rest of the tribes in the South. The Creek Nation sent an official lobbying delegation to Washington during the wars against the Native Americans in the South, but the Seminoles sent no one. The other tribes eventually signed a treaty with the United States, but not the Seminoles. The Seminoles refused even to con-federate with other Creek tribes. It was a way of keeping the history of Florida Indians intact. Florida's original

Calusas, Tequestas, and others disappeared into extinction seventy-five years before the Trail of Tears. In typical fashion, the Trail of Tears has gone on to become a landmark event in the history of the South and of the nation. It has become the subject of entire libraries of studies, while the names of Florida's original peoples are virtually unknown except to the specialist. Natives in Florida became a racial mixture of imported black slaves, Georgia Creek runaways, Spanish colonists and cracker rednecks, all amalgamated into an unlikely yet colorful mixture known as Seminoles. Florida looks different, sounds different, has a different beginning, Spanish rather than English, and has Seminoles who saw themselves as unlike other Southern tribes.

Florida does not make or grow things that remind others of the South. Georgia's peaches are virtually synonymous with Southern femininity. The Southern drawl is as sweet and slow as molasses from Louisiana cane fields; Virginia's apples, South Carolina's rice, Tennessee's corn are all Southern, if not as quintessentially so as North Carolina's tobacco, Kentucky's bluegrass, or Mississippi's cotton. Mention any one of those products anywhere in the world, even where the same crops are produced, and the crop in combination with the name of the state will likely evoke a vivid image of the South. Egypt has long produced world-class cotton, but "cotton" does not summon visions of Egypt. That is left to the pyramids. "Cotton" means Mississippi. Florida, on the other hand, has oranges, the very word of Persian, not Anglo-Saxon derivation. Oranges are not native to the South. They were introduced by the least Anglo-Saxon element of all, the Spanish. It would scarcely be less Southern as an identifying element of Florida if somehow oranges could be construed to be Catholic, rather than reliably Anglo-Saxon Protestant. Oranges are not a key ingredient of any Southern recipe, like hominy, or brunswick stew, chitlins, cornbread, or barbecue. Ambrosia, a fixture on the Thanksgiving table, must have been a northern invention on Southern tables. Oranges are more essential to Cuban cooking than to plantation feasts. Oranges are exotic as the South is exotic, but oranges are not exotic in the Southern way. Southern exotic is the pungent magnolia in blossom. Under its dark edges, Southern exotic is gothic, not Latin, sunny, or Caribbean in flavor like oranges. Oranges are exotic in an otherworldly, perhaps even oriental manner. If oranges were as Southern as watermelons or peanuts, Florida would acquire more acceptance from the rest of the South. But this is the fault of history, not of Florida.

Did Florida get shortchanged in the number of Waffle Houses across the panhandle and down the peninsula? Does Florida have too few acres under the cultivation of kudzu? Are fewer portions of grits served here per capita? Is more chardonnay and sangria instead of sweet iced tea and bourbon poured here? Is there too much hibiscus, bougainvillea, allamanda and ixora in Florida, and too little magnolia, Confederate jasmine, Cherokee rose? Can Florida have soul in the sense so readily granted to other states of the South? What is Southern is a love of the fields of home, so strong that it once overcame the good sense to relinquish slavery; a love of home so strong that it led to war. That Southerness was in the blood; it sank into the sand wherever those soldiers fell; it is a part of the makeup of those who spring from that soil, though it surfaces in vastly different ways. Florida's population today certainly does not reflect the origins of the state's earlier generations, but the blood shed for the love of the

South is not an element that bleaches out of the soil over time. Northerners are still heard complaining that Southerners should get over that war, a lesson learned from Henry Ford. But even Ford knew that history is not a lesson that one gets beyond, at least not forever. It is forever there, buried under a veneer of modernity that has obscured not just the tangible reminders of history, but has also clouded much of natural Florida that once accompanied that history.

Throughout much of the South, being Southern is a serious matter. Does Florida not take itself seriously enough to identify with the more nearly prototypical South? When Yankee tourists signaled their intention to come, Florida put its differences aside and promptly prepared, building the highways, roadside parks, motels and beach ramps for them. Florida offered only 748 miles of paved highway in 1924; but railway travel was giving way to the automobile, and so, by 1928, it had paved 2,242 miles. When it seemed the will of the rest of the country to bring segregation to an end, Florida hesitated, but then moderated. Recalcitrance just does not seem to be sustainable, in a world where sunny beaches beckon. Even the energy necessary to play hardball loses some of its competitive edge. The venerable old Southeastern Conference of university football teams provided the perfect Southern playing fields for rivalry and all its members rose long ago to positions of domination at one time or another. Georgia, Alabama, Mississippi, Tennessee, Kentucky, Louisiana—all except Florida, which finally, in 1996, after half a century of membership during which the other states' teams in turn enjoyed dominion, roused itself to a level of Southern competition sufficient to dominate. Florida was the last of the teams to do so.

It must seem that the most southerly place in the world, in the words of the *Encyclopaedia Britannica* in 1911, would, by virtue of its southernmost location, also be the most Southern place. The intensity of the heat, sunshine, hard grit of beach sand, bugs, and humidity should have highlighted the Southern aspects of Florida. As the South is to the nation, as the Delta is to the South, Florida is to the South, the most Southern of places. But Florida did not surrender its Southerness in order to invent a wholly new paradigm of state images. It has thus far replaced Southerness for an image of the great national sandbox. With all its distinctive history and unique natural beauty, it should have been possible for the advent of Pascua Florida 500, the quincentenary of Ponce de León's discovery of Florida on Easter, 1513, to bring to Florida a new image, an image not necessarily devoid of the harder and softer edges of its Southern past.

First published in *Southern Studies: An Interdisciplinary Journal of the South*, IX:I (Spring 1998), 69-85.

7

"This Ruined Landscape": Harry Crews' Florida

Of Harry Crews' fourteen novels, three are set in South Georgia and one in New Orleans, settings altogether familiar in discussions of Southern fiction. But the rest are set in Florida, and though Florida is a part of the geographic South, the writing there is not much included in discussions of Southern literature. Setting his Florida novels in hotels, gymnasiums, karate studios and soap manufacturers' offices in such hitherto unliterary places as Clearwater, Ft. Lauderdale, Jacksonville and, above all Miami Beach, makes Crews quintessentially Florida, but thus not likely to be categorized as a part of Southern fiction. Florida may be tidewater in the geophysical sense, but as a literary landscape it is hardly Tidewater, and not even the peculiar genius of Harry Crews has changed that.

It is provocative to wonder whether that is because of his idiolectal style and characters, peculiar even by Southern norms, or because of his Florida settings. Though his characters are mostly native to their settings, and his work is usually characterized as Southern in the national media, his Florida settings apparently work against Crews in securing a place in the most formal arenas of criticism of typically Southern literature. While established Southern writers have wintered in Florida as gladly as any snowbird, writers who actually live there do not form much of a part in the discussion of Southern literature. That silence includes Crews, despite thirty years writing about characters indigenous to the places they come from in various locations throughout the state.

Though he has been the subject of considerable analysis, there is in the criticism usually the suggestion that while Crews' fiction is at least nominally Southern, Florida itself is too different to fit the traditional mode of the Southern landscape that forms the core of Southern fiction.

Had he remained in his native Georgia he might more likely have written in the tradition of authors like Carson McCullers and Flannery O'Connor. But what Southern literature seems to be about, in one sense, is that regional identity is not a characteristic that can be successfully surrendered, even when in Florida's case it has been muted by change.

Much of the north of the state was once like the rest of the Deep South, as Harry Crews has observed. But the erosion of traditional Southern communities that had begun to happen in south Florida even before Crews arrived in north Florida in 1940 radically altered most of Florida, leaving only isolated remnants of an easily recognized Dixie once observable everywhere in the northern tier of counties and the Panhandle. But Crews' characters rely on much the same problems connecting family to land as characters in most Southern fiction experience; if they seem different, perhaps it is because they are in the state in the South that has continued to experience frontierlike change right on through the twentieth century, rather than like the more settled places of traditional Southern folk, where a feeling of isolation from advancing time has been one of the hallmarks of the fiction about those places.

Florida was home to very few people at a time when the other states of the South reached populations that might be thought of as their modern levels of maturity, neither radically larger nor smaller in relation to each other than they had long been. From these levels those states have continued to grow more moderately and evenly than Florida's. Little of Florida's experience during the years of the Southern renascence in the last century has been moderate. The Florida experience has all been more explosive than regular and evenly paced. But that does not metamorphose the Floridians who become Crews' characters into something other than Southerners, however much the altered landscape disguises them.

Other areas of the South have only recently experienced the tradition-altering economy, culture, and population that began to take on monumental proportions in Florida in the fifteen interstitial years between Marjorie Rawlings' death in 1953 and the publication of Harry Crews' first book in 1968. But even the literature of earlier, more traditionally Southern Florida prior to Crews—Edith Pope, Edwin Granberry, Zora Neale Hurston, Leon Odell Griffith, Rubylea Hall, Wesley Davis, or even Marjorie Kinnan Rawlings, for example—has not been widely read as a contribution to Southern fiction.

There is now a body of fiction of dark comedy, utterly appropriate to contemporary Florida, by Charles Willeford, Carl Hiaasen and others, most importantly Harry Crews, but which is still not treated critically as Southern. So whether in the earlier years of the Southern renascence or more recently, writing about Florida is not, like the literature of any other area of the South, readily thought of as belonging to Southern fiction. As different as New Orleans is, its literature is considered a part of Southern literature. It is as though Florida as a setting constituted an entirely separate genre, not as unlike mainstream as romance, or science fiction, or detective fiction, but not mainstream Southern fiction either. Yet Crews' characters struggle with many of the same tensions as other Southern characters, if not in a place that comes easily to mind among the most Southern-feeling landscapes. Just as Florida has throughout this century not found a comfortable niche in the South to which it belongs, so Crews hasn't found much of one in discussions of specifically Southern fiction. His Florida is a place set apart from other fictional Southern landscapes, as though it were the South of a country called The South.

The move to Florida from Georgia was not Crews' choice but his mother's, who fled an abusive husband on a South Georgia farm for Jacksonville, where employment in the King Edward Cigar factory made it possible even in the 1940s for a single female parent to sustain a family. But the transition from Georgia to Florida over the St. Marys river was understood to be important and therefore not allowed to go unnoticed by then five year-old Harry Crews: "Wake up and look at that," [his mother] said. "It's the border keeping Georgia and Florida separate.... It was a magic moment for me because I'd always been fascinated with boundaries and borders" (*A Childhood: The Biography of a Place*, 127), though he couldn't have imagined how the giving way of his Georgia childhood to the Florida scenes of his adult life would reverberate in his fiction.

The Crews family's migration south to Florida was not uncommon in those days. The Jacksonville to which his mother refugeed in 1940 "was filled to overflowing with South Georgia dirt farmers looking for work, looking to sell their sweat and callused hands, because that was all they had to sell" (*Scar Lover*, 20). There, like the protagonist of *Scar Lover*, "he recognized [a] voice as the voice of his people, flat, nasal, with hard r's, a voice that had drifted down into Jacksonville, Florida, out of the pine flats of south Georgia" (14). He had left behind him the language of his Georgia childhoods—eating a "slisure" of grapefruit (*Childhood*, 124), playing "marvels" with his own shooter (*Childhood*, 135), reveling in the availability of "commodity" (*Childhood*, 122). He would grow up in Florida to understand that "the hardest thing in the world was to tell somebody something, to make them know, to spread words wisely" (*Naked in Garden Hills*, 172). To the critics, the words of Crews' Florida characters constitute a separate world, unlike easily recognized Southerners elsewhere in fiction, in part at least as a result of this relocation to the less traditionally literary landscape of Florida.

Florida's terrain seems to malfunction at the very outset, the extreme northeast corner where Crews first arrived in the state. The east coast from Maine to Georgia is a series of estuarine indentations formed by east and southeast flowing rivers. But once in Florida, out of that flat landscape the state's greatest river, the St. Johns, flows first unnaturally north and then, for Florida, equally unnaturally east, emptying into the Atlantic. Not another river flows into the Atlantic along the entire four hundred fifty miles of Florida's modestly gibbous east coast. Florida depends westward and southward, and all the rivers of Florida, except the St. Johns, flow to the Gulf of Mexico: the Perdido, Escambia, Choctawhatchee, Econfina, Apalachicola, Ochlocknee, Aucilla, Wakulla, Fenholloway, Steinhatchee, Suwannee, Waccassa, Withlacoochee, Crystal, Hillsborough, Myakka, Peace, Manatee, and Caloosahatchee—all but the St. Johns.

It does not help the literary aspirations of that wayward literary landscape that on the banks of the St. Johns was written the least Southern book since the division of north from south—*Uncle Tom's Cabin*. However good the location may have been for Harriet Beecher Stowe, it has proved no panacea to Florida writers' hopes for honors in Southern fiction despite Crews' memorably shocking description of it. For though it is the grandest of Florida waterways, Harry Crews sees in Florida's mightiest river landscape only the "roiling excremental flow of the Saint John's River. Ten feet of gasoline on top of fifty feet of shit" (*Car*, 3). The pollution there gives off a distinctly unSouthern flavor. But it is the automobile and the men who drive them who have succeeded in despoiling what might have been an idyllic Southern literary flavor of the river and of Florida in Crews' novels. The real horror, though, is the extent to which his characters, failing to appreciate natural Florida, come to love what man has made of Florida, famous for four hundred years of New World history as utterly pristine, but now neatly laid out for the automobile: "It was like finding out that your son liked to hang around public restrooms smelling the toilets, or that perhaps he was secretly eating shit" (*Car*, 28). As a place ruined by the automobile, Florida, like America, is "a V-8 country, gas-driven and water-cooled, and...it belonged to men who belonged to cars" (*Car*, 79). The reaction should be, though, not that it isn't very Southern, but that it is unfortunately a precursor of the South to come, including the literary landscape now rapidly being paved over.

But the St. Marys River border had been crossed and Harry Crews became a writer of Florida, which he acknowledged, in his own unusual way: "There," he cried. "That penis [for he was a bright young man] hanging off the belly of the continent Florida" (*Naked in Garden Hills*, 11), cries the protagonist of Crews' very first novel set in Florida, establishing the anatomical likeness as a metaphor for much of what is worst, though not less Southern, in his characters. Crews has continued since to create Southern fiction in this most difficult place to recognize traditional Southern trappings: "most of Crews' books are set in that peculiar state," Jonathan Yardley cheekily observed in the *Washington Post* "Bookworld" in 1993. And Yardley has not been alone in connecting Crews to his uncomfortable settings. An earlier critic discerns almost apologetically that Crews "comes from a poor rural background in southern Georgia, and finds himself uneasy in urban Florida, a greater dislocation than most northerners might credit," said Gregory Feeley in the *Washington Post* "Bookworld" in 1992. Crews' most articulate critic, Frank Shelton, describes Crews' settings as the "commercialized, vulgarized South of modem Florida, where tradition is nonexistent" ("Man's Search for Perfection," *The Southern Literary Journal*, 99). More apocalyptically still, a reader observes that "What man has created of it, the reclamation sites, the strips of beach and highway north of Miami, the car terminals like Jacksonville, have nothing godly residing in them as places" (Jack Moore, *A Grit's Triumph: Essays on the Works of Harry Crews*, 59).

How, indeed, does such a place ever succeed as the setting of serious novels? How, one wonders, can Florida be so devoid of appeal to all but tourists in search of the popular, so alien to the artist, yet still call forth from this gifted writer of fiction ten distinguished books? Crews himself offers something of an answer: "I like to start with something that is obviously a world that nobody can quarrel with. Here is the porch and there is the chair and here is the man.... Then in a very slow kind of left-handed way...it just slides off the edge of the real world into a thing that can't possibly be true...to distort the real world in order to be able to render accurately and truly the psychological reality and emotional reality of people in his age" (Joe David Bellamy, "Harry Crews: An Interview," *Fiction International*, 92). The resulting emotional and psychological landscapes, while removed from traditional Southern realism, suggest something of scenes to come for Southerners everywhere in this fast changing landscape.

Setting for Crews isn't just a matter of fidelity to location, but also of time, exacerbated by the pace of change man is asked to endure and absorb. One of Crews' most intense characters serves as a model, living as he does by "the stopwatch. He felt better the moment he touched it. For him it was a kind of metaphor that contained everything clean, lucid and ultimately understandable…. You could not bullshit a stopwatch" (*All We Need of Hell*, 43). The stilled time of the past seems unable to influence the pace of the present. Crews has lived thirty years within a few miles of Rosewood, without ever having mentioned that place. The landscape no longer moors us, and thus "place in Crews' fiction is carefully designed to help dramatize that world from which God seems to have departed.... Crews stresses the harshness and ugliness of its terrain...a bleak and bitter and unproductive land... a newer, tawdry South without rich traditions" (Jack Moore, *A Grit's Triumph*, 65). His fiction never seems to invest much, even in his Georgia novels, in traditional usages of place alone to engender stories growing out of the land, but is more concerned with how increasingly difficult it becomes to make that connection.

The Georgia of his childhood, so inviting a setting for a Southerner's stories, is the scene in some of his novels of such recognizably Southern tableaux as gospel sings, rattlesnake roundups, and rocking chairs on the front porch of an old folks home. Crews' Florida, on the other hand, appears at first reading as a place only of the pageants defined in Webster's as "mere show," "pretense," "ostentatious display," "an elaborate colorful spectacle," but which Crews reminds us is the place we now live, convincing us that stories happen in just such unlikely settings. Though Crews writes of Bacon County, Georgia, as a place where extreme hardship is a source of great Southern storytelling, he writes equally convincingly of Miami: "You can't tell a story that hasn't happened here and won't happen again" (*The Mulching of America*, 118).

The best Southern literary settings are traditionally rural and isolated, like Faulkner's famous postage stamp-sized area, or, in Florida, of Marjorie Rawlings' tiny, remote Cross Creek. Crews takes scenes from all over Florida, even its largest cities, and creates a similar isolation within the multitudes of those cities. Just as in Southern literature's familiar regard for hometown as place, Crews reinforces our isolation in the expansiveness of Florida by diminishing his portion of it down to a mere "5 foot radius around wherever I happen to be standing" (*Karate is a Thing of the Spirit*, 150). In constricting the relationship between his characters and their places through ten Florida novels, Crews has created a world that, since it is vacationland Florida, might have been expected to appeal to Hollywood filmmakers more than to readers of Southern fiction. His freaks in their peculiar landscapes have thus far defied Hollywood casting directors, perhaps because they are more deserving of Gustave Dore than of Steven Spielberg. But they have not yet had much discussion as Southerners, either.

Though the two states enjoy two hundred miles of proximity over a barely distinguishable border, Florida and Georgia are, in fairness to those who see little of the South in the Florida in Crews' novels, utterly separate places. Georgia is, of course, one of the likeliest places for Southern literature to happen. Waycross, for instance, is the kind of place where the real names of real characters "is caught hard to blood" (*Body,* 64), whereas Miami Beach is the kind of place where characters end up on the fifteenth floor: "Hell of a thing living on the fifteenth floor of a hotel, the fifteenth floor of anything. It ain't many white men and no niggers at all that'd want to live that high in the air. Ain't natural" (*Body,* 36). In the novels with Georgia settings the characters belong in obvious ways to the land and the family. In the Florida novels the characters seem to belong more to the pageant, the stage, the show, the spectacle. The characters in the Georgia novels suffer isolation, but one of the elements isolating them is the suffocating familiarity of a home place they can't escape. In the Florida novels, the characters are dislocated by, among other problems, the lack of familiarity with a place to which they obviously belong. The scenes are never home, or any other natural setting, but rather a gym, a hotel, an automobile graveyard, a phosphate pit, an upholstery shop. The names of the towns in Georgia are fictional, so that the entire setting is lifted to the level of metaphor—Mystic, Cumseh, Enigma (Enigma is real, but Crews apparently assumes no reader beyond Georgia, or the South, would ever believe it). The names of the Florida towns are not fictional, but absolutely literal—Miami, Tampa, Gainesville, Jacksonville, Ft. Lauderdale. Florida, Crews reasons, is sufficiently fantastic, or bizarre, not to need fictional names in order to seem fictional. But bizarre is not antithetical to what makes a setting Southern.

It is doubtless emblematic, in fourteen novels clearly separated into the landscapes of the two adjacent states, that the highest level of abstraction in any of the Georgia titles is the less than optimistic reminder that *This Thing Don't Lead to Heaven*, but the equally highest level of abstraction among Florida titles abandons even the hope of ambiguity to offer the reader the dismaying assurance that this is, indeed, *All We Need of Hell*. A Georgia character knows that a "man wouldn't want to come off down here amongst all these people who ain't normal in any way that counts..." (*Body*, 125). But his Florida characters know that "If you're going to be anything or know anything or do anything, you've got to be abnormal. Whatever's normal is a loss. Normal is for shit" (*The Hawk is Dying*, 165). In crossing the St. Marys border Crews forfeits the easy place in Southern literature almost assured by a

South Georgia setting for a place entirely his own, but one that is a part of the South even if it is hard to recognize as such. Southern literature offers diversity enough to include such disparate places as Yoknapatawpha, Peter Taylor's Tennessee urbanity, Styron's aristocratic Tidewater and O'Connor's Georgia, even diverse enough for many readers for that literature to embrace Harry Crews' Florida.

Every Southern chamber of commerce probably covets its very own *Gone With the Wind* to put it forever on the travel map. Art being less than the flatterer it is often mistaken for, not every place lucks into a flatterer the equal in the affections of readers of Margaret Mitchell as its chronicler. Charleston and The Citadel have been illustrated by Pat Conroy but have not always been happy, even with admissions up. Columbus was not always thrilled with Carson McCullers. Most towns, at least their chambers of commerce, doubtless hope for writers endowed not so keenly with truth as with flattery. But some of the towns in Florida have been among the least—and, perhaps, also among the most— enviable of all. They are known worldwide for their attractions, but to seekers of the real Florida they are known because of Harry Crews. The eschatological goings-on Crews describes in Miami, Ft. Lauderdale, Clearwater, Jacksonville, and Gainesville wouldn't likely have taken place in more traditionally Southern places like Natchez, Charleston, or Milledgeville, at least not as they have thus far been depicted in fiction. But Crews suggests that the grand Southern finale could as likely be played out in a site not unlike the Blue Flamingo Hotel in Miami as in the Mississippi Delta.

Southern writers are visceral about place, but love the redeeming qualities of the places they write about. Harry

Crews hates what his characters have done to their places, down the entire length of the peninsula from Jacksonville, "sinkhole for the castoffs and drags of Georgia" (Robert Sherrill, *The New York Times* "Book Review," 1978) all the way to Miami, "what it's gonna be like to live out your life in this old crooked and tainted world without a dream" (*Mulching*, 224). These literary landscapes serve Crews as visible reminders of the conditions of modern life that enrage him, and should all of us, not only the familiar Southern problems of the outrages of racism and poverty, discriminate health care and education, but also the ransom of civility by the automobile, and the disfiguring urban sprawl, problems now on their way to every corner of the South. Crews offers the theme of obsession with place familiar in Southern writing, but Crews' characters experience a dissociation and alienation exacerbated, rather than ameliorated, by place. Florida's distinctive shape, the flaccid one of Crews' image, seems to have been the landscape Crews knows himself to have been destined for, "walking," like Pete Butcher, "with a strange calmness now that it somehow felt as though he had finally come to the place he had been headed all his life" (*Scar Lover*, 118). Crews writes of a recognizable Georgia, but the Florida he writes of is not so recognizable as a real place as it is a landscape in his fertile imagination; "the only place I'm from is wherever I happen to find myself standing" (Bellamy 86).

Georgia is for Crews the kind of Southern place "where blood is joined...the place where the blood that beats in one heart beats in another" (*Scar Lover*, 129), while Florida is but a place where "there ain't a tree that don't have a light on it or ain't held up by a stick" (*Mulching*, 30). But it does not finally matter in Harry Crews' landscapes which way rivers flow or that trees are of recent planting. Southern literary staples of geographical verisimilitude are not important here. Harry Crews makes the reader suspect that Southern writers spoil us with lavish attention to the landscape, the South itself, contours so lovingly sculpted in fiction that they become the equal of the characters who inhabit them. But in the novels of Harry Crews, the character of Florida has not been the equal of the characters who live there but has been overwhelmed by them. Crews tells a disturbing story of a Florida where man has not been made better through loyalty to the land but has despoiled the land for his convenience, of a scene close to ruin as a result of our lack of stewardship, but one not confined to Florida.

Originally published in *The Marjorie Kinnan Rawlings Journal of Florida Literature*, VIII (1999), 39-48.

8

Edith Pope's *Colcorton*

Florida seems always to have been home to the unusual, but in all five hundred years of its recorded history Florida has produced few more engaging or elusive personalities than Zephaniah Kingsley who, though a leading slave trader, married more than one of his slaves, and spent his adult life laboring for better treatment of blacks, both slave and free.

Born in Scotland in 1765, Kingsley arrived in Florida in 1803 and was soon the most prominent slave trader in the state if not much of the entire South. Foreign slave trade was outlawed in the United States by 1808, but in Spanish Florida Kingsley was free to continue to import slaves. His home at the mouth of the St. Johns River, surviving today as a national park, is probably the oldest extant plantation home in Florida. Appointed by President Monroe to the Legislative Council which governed Florida after its absorption into the United States under territorial status, Kingsley chaired the committee which selected Tallahassee as the state capitol, midway between the two centers of population in Pensacola and St. Augustine. He was not reappointed to the Legislative Council, as other councilors routinely were, because of his advocacy of civil rights for freed slaves. A speech by Kingsley promoting those rights is the only language to survive in the archives from the second convening of the Florida Council. Kingsley married four of his African slaves and set them up in separate plantation households along the St. Johns. He wrote a will bequeathing them their properties and their freedom; he set up a colony for freed slaves in less race-conscious Haiti; he wrote and frequently revised a widely distributed pamphlet encouraging better treatment of slaves, and worked all his life as a Floridian to promote that end.

The paradoxical life of the Scotsman transplanted to frontier Florida who simultaneously bought and sold slaves, yet worked to promote humane treatment of them, is a story that has proved attractive but elusive for Florida writers. Marjorie Kinnan Rawlings, at the urging of Kingsley authority Philip May, labored to find a way into a story that would endow the Zephaniah Kingsley legend with enduring metaphor. Other Florida writers were similarly drawn to the intriguing inconsistencies of the Kingsley story. Only one writer, Edith Pope, succeeded in creating a narrative capable of burnishing the legacy of the contradictory Kingsley. Creating a story ostensibly of the mixed-blood offspring of Kingsley and his African wives, thus removing the setting from the time actually surrounding Kingsley's own life, Edith Pope's novel makes not only a much needed contribution to Florida's role in the Southern literary renascence but extends Kingsley's racial concerns.

Her story is the novel *Colcorton*, an important contribution to the theme of racial discord in a region thrumming with virulent segregationist sentiment soon after Pope's novel first appeared in 1944 to congratulatory reviews. The charm of Florida's northeastern corner, from the mouth of the St. Johns River to historic, quaint St. Augustine, the setting of *Colcorton*, had been disturbed with racial incidence more often than today's tourist economy would suggest. The black nursemaid of the grandchildren of Henry Seidel Canby, founder of *The Saturday Review of Literature*, was arrested in 1953, less than a decade after the publication of *Colcorton* and the year before Pope's last novel was published, for an early morning swim at the whites-only beach at St. Augustine. In 1958, the mother of Massachusetts Governor Endicott Peabody was arrested at a St. Augustine diner for attempting to order a meal for herself and her black servants. Martin Luther King, Jr., chose St. Augustine for the final rally for the signing of the 1964 Civil Rights Act. St. Augustine, then, is an important symbol not only of Florida's origins beginning with Juan Ponce de León, but also as a symbol of the ongoing problem of race central to American history.

Interest in Florida history encouraged Pope to work within the framework of the actual lives of Kingsley and Anna Madgigane Jai, Kingsley's slave whom he later married. But her concern with racism led Pope to a more important work of fiction by inspiring the creation of Abby Clanghearne, fictional offspring of the legendary Kingsley. Kingsley had argued in 1821 as a member of the Legislative Council for the adoption of laws similar to medieval Spanish race laws, long in effect in Florida during the centuries of Spanish rule, encouraging incorporation of freed slaves into society as a third class, between whites and slaves. His pamphlet writing beginning in 1828 set forth reasons for more humane attitudes towards blacks. But the Florida Council, made up of planters migrating to Florida from elsewhere in the South, adopted instead even more restrictive laws barring free blacks from entering Florida. Slaves freed within the state could have no civil freedoms and could be sold back into slavery without the protection of their previous owner. Kingsley's will encouraged his family to escape to "some land of liberty and equal rights, where the conditions of society are governed by some law less absurd than that of color." He warned of the "illiberal and inequitable laws of this territory which will not afford to them and to their children that protection and justice [due] in every civilized society to every human being."

Kingsley had in fact already provided the haven suggested in his will, moving most of his family produced by the four African wives to Haiti beginning in 1835. He died in 1843, two years before Florida moved from territorial status to statehood, and after thirty seven years of marriage to Anna Madgigene Jai, one of his four African wives. Anna returned to her property near Jacksonville in 1846 but, as a Union supporter, fled to Philadelphia, then New York, when the Civil War began, which destroyed her Florida properties. After the war she returned to Florida and lived until 1870 with her daughters in homes along the St. Johns River in Jacksonville. Edith Pope's *Colcorton* was published almost on the centennial of Kingsley's death in New York City ninety-nine years later.

Race would have been no easy matter to gloss over by the time Edith Pope wrote *Colcorton*. By 1944 a distinguished roster of Southern novels had securely established the tradition of dealing with race, despite the popularity of Thomas Nelson Page's Old South plantation novels. T. S. Stribling's *Birthright* appeared in 1922, Jean Toomer's *Cane* in 1923, Walter White's *The Fire in the Flint* in 1924, and Dubose Heyward's *Porgy* in 1925. Julia Peterkin published *Black April* in 1927, then won the Pulitzer Prize in 1929 for *Scarlet Sister Mary*, the year that also saw the publication of Heyward's *Mamba's Daughters*. Arna Bontemp's *God Sends Sunday* told the story of black life in Louisiana in 1931. Peterkin's *Bright Skin* came in 1932, George W. Henderson's *Ollie Miss* in 1935, and Waters Turpin's *These Low Grounds*, Lyle Saxon's *Children of Strangers* and George Washington Lee's *River George* in 1937. Waters Turpin's *0 Canaan* was published in 1939, Erskine Caldwell's *Trouble in July* in 1940, as well as Richard Wright's magisterial *Native Son* and William Attaway's *Blood on the Forge*, in 1949. In Florida, where Edith Pope was serving her own long writing apprenticeship to the Zephaniah Kingsley legend, Zora Neale Hurston wrote *Jonah's Gourd Vine* in 1934, *Mules and Men* in 1935, and *Their Eyes Were Watching God* in 1936.

Set in the midst of the ongoing literary presentation of race relations, 1944 in particular brought three novels illuminating the destructiveness of racism. All three writers were white. Two were women. Hodding Carter's *The Winds of Fear* illustrated white Mississippi intellectuals struggling to make a better place for their counterpart black Mississippi intellectuals. Lillian Smith's *Strange Fruit* reversed that perception to show a black heroine in Georgia trying to cope with loving a white man who proved unworthy of her. Black characters in black society had been the medium of Toomer, Hurston, Bontemps, Henderson, Turpin, and Attaway. Caldwell,

Stribling, Smith, and Carter featured sympathetic black characters in a white milieu. Edith Pope's *Colcorton* brings the two together with the generations of the mixed blood offspring of Florida's Zephaniah Kingsley and his African princess wife Anna Madgigene Jai Kingsley. Redefining racial polarities using mulatto characters was already a steadily accumulating theme in Southern fiction, from George Washington Cable in the nineteenth century to Julia Peterkin's unusual *Bright Skin*, where a mulatto character faces a hostile black world, and Saxon's *Children of Strangers*. That tradition continued with distinction well past Edith Pope's protagonist, Abby Clanghearne, with Robert Penn Warren's *Band of Angels* in 1955.

Edith Pope's first three books suggest that she might have come to the writing of the fourth, *Colcorton*, less interested in racism than in the theme of feminism. Her fifth and final novel, *River in the Wind*, suggests now that had she written about Zephaniah Kingsley himself as a character, larger than life in antebellum, anteterritorial Florida, Pope would have been more interested in Florida as a setting than in creating her character. The decade in which she wrote *Colcorton* was in fact characterized by a remarkable number of historical novels set in Florida. But the problems faced by Abby Clanghearne, if not especially her reconciliation of them, leave little doubt that Edith Pope intended not only to reflect on the era in Florida represented by the story of her heroine, and also to make her heroine a defender of women's rights, but to condemn the problems inherited by Kingsley's offspring, and thus inherited in some way by every generation of Americans since the arrival of the first slaves.

The climate in Florida in 1944 did not suggest any likelihood of the appearance of a novel central to the race question. Nor did the events in Edith Pope's life. Florida's two historically all black towns were equidistant from her in St. Augustine, American Beach forty miles north, and Eatonville, home of Zora Neale Hurston, forty miles to the south. Nothing indicates that Edith Pope was especially conscious of American Beach, but she knew and corresponded with Hurston from Eatonville. Florida was home to less than two million people, not the twenty million of today. Cattle still freely roamed major highways, the fencing law not enacted for another five years. There was as yet no sales tax. Only half million automobile tags were sold that year. New Dealer Claude Pepper represented Florida in the United States Senate. Florida had eight seats in the Congress, none of them occupied since Reconstruction by any other than a white male. The state was no better known then as a literary center than now.

As today, Florida as a literary setting largely produced detective thrillers, though many writers wintered in Edith Pope's St. Augustine, including Thornton Wilder, James Branch Cabell, William Rose Benet, Dorothy Heyward, A. J. Cronin, and Robert Frost, among others. Though Marjorie Rawlings, Robert Wilder, Stetson Kennedy, Theodore Pratt, Edwin Granberry and others were then active writers on the Florida scene, except for *Colcorton*, the detective novel dominated the publishers list of Floridians in 1944. Brett Halliday published two Mike Shayne's that year, in addition to detective novels by Lee Thayer, Gil Brewer, and Gordon Volk. The inexplicable connection between beaches and criminals has continued with Ed McBains's Matthew Hope, Charles Willeford's Hoke Moseley, and the color-coordinated characters of John D. McDonald, a more constant theme among Florida writers than the problems of racial inequality.

By 1944 Pope was herself already the author of three novels, all studies of strong-willed women fighting the stereotypes of prescribed gender roles still in force in Pope's youth. *Not Magnolia* (1928) is the story of a young woman of Tallahassee's minor social aristocracy contending with family and social restrictions of what Pope described as the "moonlight and magnolia" attitude restricting women. *Old Lady Esteroy* (1934) presents an aging dowager who rages at the lack of men strong enough to equal her in strength of character. *Half-Holiday* (1938) is about three young wives anxiously waiting the overdue return of their husbands from a fishing trip. None of the stories of these strong women of the earlier novels suggest the power Edith Pope would find in her fourth heroine, Abby Clanghearne, mistress of Colcorton, and descendant of a fictionalized Zephaniah Kingsley and his Senegalese princess wife. The name "Clanghearne" would become a mnemonic tocsin clangorously suggestive of the racial inheritance from the more sonorously original "Kingsley."

Born Edith Everett Taylor in St. Augustine in 1905, Pope's father was an engineer from New Jersey, her mother the daughter of a northern businessman who had retired to St. Augustine. Pope spent her childhood first in a convent school, then at the Swiss high school La Perie, and at the Baldwin School in Philadelphia before matriculating at the Florida State College for Women in 1926. After college she eloped with Verle Pope of St. Augustine in 1933 and published her first novel the following year. Theirs was one of the famous "Florida divided" marriages, he a graduate of the then men-only University of Florida, she a graduate of the then women-only Florida State College. The intensity of such marriages has doubtless increased since the Pope's respective alma maters became national football rivals in 1958, four years before Pope died. Her husband Verle spent his life in politics, holding until 1972 the seat in the Florida Senate formerly occupied by her father. Verle served as president of the Florida Senate in its 1967 session. He had been considered the front-running candidate for the Democratic nomination as governor of Florida in 1960 but chose not to run because of the severity of Edith's debilitating rheumatoid arthritis. The St. Johns County seat he held in the Florida Senate played a role both in Edith Pope's life and in her fiction. Her heroine Abby Clanghearne in *Colcorton* imagines her brother Jared, newly graduated from the University of Florida law School, going on to become state senator, then governor, the same political trajectory Pope's husband and father had aspired to.

Edith Pope's *Colcorton* utilizes little of her hometown's ancient Spanish history as the oldest city in the United States, a history she would use significantly in her last novel. *Colcorton* instead grows out of the legacy of the Anglo-Saxon tradition of slave trading, more lucrative in its day than any form of commerce invented by the Spanish after plundering Mexico and Peru, or by English colonists re-making themselves as Yankee entrepreneurs. The novel echoes the warning that however lucrative slavery was for the earliest generations making a living that way, the legacy of such an economy is not financial security but a cruel racial divide. Colcorton, the house of the title and setting, while not literally in St. Johns County now, was in the first decades of the nineteenth century when the house was built, the oldest plantation home still standing in Florida. Edith Pope makes it the scene of the oldest and severest of problems in the New World, complicating the lives of her characters generations after the lives of the originals, just as the original slavery has transmogrified into its incarnation as racism.

As the novel opens, Abby Clanghearne waits at the dilapidated ancestral home, Colcorton, for her brother Jared to return from the University of Florida, a hundred miles away, where he has just completed a law degree. Abby is aware of her lineage but has contrived through self-sacrifice to keep it secret from her brother. Abby has endured great financial hardship to make Jared's education possible. She remembers him in youth as driven to succeed as she has been for him. But when he returns home from graduation, he arrives ready for relaxation, having unexpectedly brought with him a new bride, Beth, from a once-aristocratic but now land-poor old Alabama family. Abby at once worries that any children they might produce will further reveal the Negro ancestry already now beginning to show in Abby's face. She is herself in love with the upstanding backwoodsman, Danny Strikeleather, but has never married him for fear of bestowing on another generation the difficult mantle of mixed blood.

Into this household comes Edith Pope's favorite male characterization, the one man in the cast of characters in any of her books strong enough to equal her women protagonists. As in each of her earlier novels, this male character opposite her female protagonist is able to equal the heroine only because of his strength as an artist. Clement Johnson, a Yankee writer, has been thought by some readers to have been inspired by Sinclair Lewis, whom Pope knew during his sojourns in Florida, though Edith Pope's life in St. Augustine was crowded with many literary personages of northern extraction. Johnson has rented a room in Colcorton in order to write his next book. Because he is endowed with the observant artist's gift for detail, Clement Johnson sees at once, of course, the possible signs in Abby of mixed blood. Abby's travail is the story he has long sought for his elusive next novel.

One of Jared's first legal cases takes him to Tallahassee to unravel the rightful ownership of Danny Strikeleather's homestead, complicated as part of an original Spanish royal grant, but there in the archives at the capital he also inadvertently uncovers the far greater complication of his own racial heritage in the will whereby he and Abby have inherited *Colcorton*. Unable, like his sister Abby, to cope with his heritage, Jared degenerates into alcoholism and is killed in a gambling brawl. Abby is left to face the prying eyes of the artist-character Clement Johnson, ever eager for a new story to reinvent his career as a writer. Johnson begins at once turning her into his fictional character Pride McCullough, playing on Abby's fiercely proud nature as well as her real "McColor." Beth bears Jared's son, a happy child whose dancing reminds Clement Johnson of the black children he had seen dancing in Haiti: "I thought it was unique to the black race. But Jared is as good as they are" pounding out rhythm, "as if he was dancing on the jungle floor" (*Colcorton* 222). Abby confronts Johnson over her right to her privacy versus his right as an artist to any material for a good story. Johnson insists that being an artist is a harder burden to bear than her mixed blood, that they both face a world of prejudice. Edith Pope is writing out of autobiography, hers and that of many other Florida writers in search of authentic Florida stories, in having her artist-character Johnson find his next great story in that of the offspring of the slave trader Zephaniah Kingsley. Abby considers burning Colcorton in an effort to expunge in the crucible of such a fire her own racial past, but instead relents and sells it to Johnson for about the same amount as the price of one of Zephaniah Kingsley's best slaves a hundred fifty years earlier. The child Jared and his mother escape to the north on the proceeds of the sale of Colcorton. Thus Abby resolves the conflict between her privacy as opposed to the artist's right to her story as literary material in such a way that spares young Jared the ignominy of life blighted by bigotry while not denying the artist his right to his story.

At the novel's end Edith Pope draws a picture of the imagery of color in the landscape as a metaphor for the colors that have plagued her characters. At the end of her last black night at Colcorton, the dawn turns Colcorton the bleached white of "a corpse under water," a time when "no birds cry, sea oats hang limp, the sea and all else is grey," before the night returns all to blackness in a metaphor of the cyclical rather than fixed application of color that Abby Clanghearne has been unable to escape. Looking for what she expects will be a final time at Colcorton, Abby sees the last, flaking chips of white paint in the elaborate Corinthian capital at the top of its column, between prickly, spiky leaves of the thistle-like acanthus motif, the paint "all but a faint drift of chalk that was paint in its last metamorphosis" (*Colcorton* 323). She knows that "all the world (including races) was just one living thing, divided up into sky and folks and oak trees and all, but all living in God's mind.... For they was all one, and all was God" (*Colcorton* 313).

This poetic fictionalization of one of Florida's most elusive stories very nearly won the Pulitzer prize in 1945, losing to John Hersey's *A Bell for Adano* by only a single vote after multiple-ballots in which they tied. Pope had removed her characters to offspring generations after the epochal lives of Anna Madgigene Jai and Zephaniah Kingsley, knowing that to attempt a saga of proportions proper to the original generation would put her story directly in the path of the 1936 juggernaut of Civil War epics, *Gone With the Wind*, as much the Dixie Limited for Civil War epicists as Flannery O'Connor opined of Southern writers in William Faulkner's path. Pope might reasonably have thought of 1945 as another southern woman's turn at the Pulitzer. Julia Peterkin had won for *Scarlet Sister Mary* 1929, Caroline Miller in 1934 for *Lamb in His Bosom*, Margaret Mitchell in 1936, Marjorie Kinnan Rawlings in 1939, and Ellen Glasgow in 1942. 1945 must have looked promising to her with this breakthrough novel on race. Paul Robeson was the Spingarn medalist in 1945. Bess Myerson was Miss America. The war ended. Cordell Hull won the Nobel Peace prize. "The Lost Weekend" swept the Oscars. In other Pulitzers Karl Shapiro won for poetry, "Appalachian Spring" for music, "Harvey" for drama, Bill Mauldin for cartooning. The Nobel for literature went to Chilean Gabriela Mistral, who had spent 1939 at 24 Avenida Menendez, only doors down the street from Edith Pope's St. Augustine home during the very writing of *Colcorton*.

Without an older literary tradition in the European style, American literature claims no single indisputable epic. Critics have been unable to agree conclusively to designate any one book the Great American Novel, despite numerous good choices in a genre at which American writers have excelled.

Titles that have endured in the search for the best, from *The Adventures of Huckleberry Finn* to *The Sound and the Fury* to *The Confessions of Nat Turner*, deal with race. Despite having dominated throughout much of the twentieth century, Southern literature is as yet unsure exactly which of Faulkner's or Warren's or Wolfe's books is best, or to decide which is the great Civil War novel, despite the enormous popularity of one in particular. The best might be, critics hesitate to say, *So Red the Rose*, or *None Shall Look Back*, or *The Killer Angels*, or *The Fathers*, or even *Bugles Blow No More*. The central event in American history maintains its popularity in fiction with *Cold Mountain*. A subject indistinguishable from the Civil War, distinguished by its own long list of titles of renown, is race. Edith Pope set her own high water mark in *Colcorton*, her paean to the long past in Florida, a state that has known its share of the amalgams of Spanish, French, British, Caribbean, Native American, cracker, and African American. She went on to write a fifth and final novel, *River in the Wind*, a sweeping epic of Florida in the Seminole Wars, crowded with all the historical figures of those years. But neither it nor any of her first three novels is the compelling Florida tale that *Colcorton* is, celebrating in the legend of Zephaniah Kingsley the legacy of one of the most enigmatic figures in all of Florida history.

Originally published in *The Marjorie Kinnan Rawlings Journal of Florida Literature*, XIX (2011), 99-110.

9

Florida Politics: Ambition in the Balmy Latitudes

One of Florida's most eminent historians, Charlton Tebeau, wrote in 1980, updating his 1971 *History of Florida*:

> Politics promises to be far more lively in the future. Now that Florida is the ninth state in the Union in population, the stakes are higher, and the partisan rivalry may be expected to produce a doubly exciting show. From recent quardicentennials—commemorating the de Luna effort to settle Pensacola in 1559, the Ribault visit to the Saint Johns River in 1562, the establishment of Fort Caroline by the French near the mouth of the Saint Johns River in 1564, and the founding of Saint Augustine in 1565—reminded the country and the world of the antiquity of Florida's heritage. Contemporary Floridians have announced their bid for a larger place in the world of the future. (152)

The seaboard South had seventy-five years of governance practice. Florida got a good start, but merely a dozen years in the Union, joined the Confederacy, and within days sent a Secretary of the Navy to Richmond. Back in the US, and the twentieth century, Florida eventually provided an Attorney General, a Secretary of Commerce, a Broadcasting Secretary, trade representatives, an envoy to Latin America and such distinguished chairs of major committees as Claude Pepper, Dante Fascell, and C.W. Young. But in the long roll-call of presidents, vice presidents, speakers, and Supreme Court justices, Florida's role seems small except, lately, in numbers of electoral votes.

One reason sometimes cited for Florida's lack of participation in politics at the national level is the widely held misperception that Florida became part of the Union long after other Southern states. The South is an old part of the Union, nearly half the states having been among the original thirteen English-speaking colonies. But Florida's admission to statehood in 1845 did not occur for fifty years after the beginning of federal government. During that half century before Florida's admission, from 1789 to 1845, the other Southern states enjoyed the benefits of seventy-five national leaders, including eight presidents, four vice presidents, fourteen justices of the Supreme Court, twelve speakers of the House of Representatives, and seven cabinet officers. Throughout the century after Florida joined the Union, from 1845 to 1945, during which time Florida presumably had an equal chance with the rest of the South, the other Southern states elected or otherwise enjoyed the prestige of having virtually as many as they had had in the half-century before Florida's admission, sixty-six national leaders, including four presidents, five vice presidents, eight speakers of the House, twenty-two justices of the Supreme Court, and twenty-eight cabinet officers, but still none from Florida. Florida was actually closer to councils of national governance before becoming a state. Andrew Jackson, after his military governorship organizing Florida into a territory, appointed his associate, John Eaton, to be Florida's second territorial governor, then subsequently made him Secretary of War, then Minister to Spain. Jackson appointed John Branch sixth territorial governor of Florida and, subsequently, Secretary of the Navy. From Jackson's presidency to Attorney General Reno, no one with Florida connections has been as close to national power as those officials of pre-statehood Territorial Florida.

Traditionally the proud Southerner cites Virginia's role as mother of presidents. But the rest of the South, exclusive of Florida, had its share of men connected to high office during those same years. Aside from Virginia's seven presidents, Georgia had benefited from the connections of fifteen such eminences, including a president, three speakers of the House, thirteen cabinet officers, and four Supreme Court Justices. Tennessee has provided nineteen luminaries, including four presidents and six justices. The Carolinas have enjoyed the prestige of eleven national officers, including vice presidents, justices, speakers, and cabinet officers. Even Louisiana, Alabama, and Mississippi, the triumvirate of the lowest, deepest South, have known dozens of national political leaders, including six Supreme Court justices. Florida has never benefited from connection to national power equal to those states, or to almost any of the states elsewhere in the union.

In the early decades of the republic, Florida could not match the political strength of even the newer states west of the Mississippi. Twenty-two of the twenty-three western states have enjoyed better connections to national political stature. Only two of those twenty-two states are older than

Florida. Four of them haven't been states throughout all of the twentieth century, but those four have already sent to Washington secretaries of Agriculture, Interior, and War, speakers of the House, Senate floor leaders, attorneys general, and justices of the Supreme Court. Five states without coastlines have sent Secretaries of the Navy to Washington. The apolitical nature of Florida politics, with respect to national levels of activity, suggests that Florida and Hawaii constitute a virtually separate union, both relegated to playground status. Among political axioms, apparently, if the weather is pleasant, the people enjoying it will not likely be serious about politics. Florida still awaits the actual election of one of its own to national office. In one hundred fifty years of statehood, no one nurtured in Florida politics has ever held any position higher than member of the cabinet.

It is as though political office in Florida, especially the governorship, were so exalted a position that no holder of that office could ever aspire to higher. Neither the governorship nor the seats in Congress has led to a political dynasty like Mississippi's Bilbos or Percys, Georgia's Talmadges, Louisiana's Longs, or Virginia's Byrds. Those dynasties have been mixed blessings to those states, adding power and patronage but finally detracting from their reputation for political sophistication. Florida has not enjoyed a reputation for sophistication in exchange for its lack of leverage in Washington. While it is perhaps lucky for Florida that the 1967 campaign of irrepressible Governor Claude Kirk for the vice presidential nomination on the Republican ticket failed, no Florida political leader otherwise has had sufficient energy to dominate the scene long enough, or to fashion a career obviously intended to result in a national office. Jeb Bush was ambushed by Donald Trump.

Florida was served once by a politician accomplished at the art of political spin long before television commentators began offering that by-product of political rhetoric on a regular, predictable basis. He campaigned successfully in his rural, backwater home county by announcing to the voters there that his opponent, the incumbent, walked the streets of the capital as a practicing homo sapiens, though the rascal had managed to keep that revealing fact from voters back home. Such inspired campaigning, doubtless necessary to achieve position of national power, must be the equal in chicanery of any trick served up by politicians throughout the rest of the South. By AD 2000, Virginia, Tennessee, Georgia, and Arkansas will have accounted for seventy-five years of the two hundred twelve years of governance in the office of president alone, and more than twice that many, with vice presidents included, since the founding of the republic. But no Floridians have ever surfaced in the highest sweepstakes.

There was a brief moment when LeRoy Collins had served an enlightened tenure as governor and had gone on to minor prominence as an appointee in Washington—clearly on his way to higher levels of office holding, despite (in Florida) or because (nationally) of his participation in the celebrated march from Selma, Alabama. Almost as if to confirm his ascendancy, Collins was designated keynote speaker at a national Democratic convention. But in the middle of his forthright and thoughtful address, which could have propelled him to attention as a possible vice presidential candidate, former First Lady Eleanor Roosevelt was escorted into the hall and to her seat, setting off such enthusiastic response among loyalists wistful for happier days as to completely distract jubilant Democrats from the remarks of their keynoter. Collins subsequently lost a race for the United States Senate that might have rehabilitated his career.

Before LeRoy Collins' interrupted remarks there had been talk in 1960 of Senator George Smathers as John Kennedy's choice of vice presidential running mates. The irony of such rumors prefigures the sad state of Florida politics in general. Had Smathers been Kennedy's choice he would have become vice president, and Florida would have leaped over all the other lesser offices of national leadership in the trajectory to the top, becoming president in the wake of the assassination. A native son would have become president without the long wait up through the ranks.

Florida does not seem ever in its long English-speaking history to have been an aggressively political place, at least not with any grand design on influencing national affairs. Before the coming of Americans and English, the royal courts of France and Spain intrigued constantly over Florida. Jean Ribaut and Pedro Menéndez de Avilés were among the ablest men France and Spain could summon for the project of furthering their interests in the New World. But since both of those great powers of the Europe of their day retreated in the eighteenth century, leaving the field to speakers of English, native-bred politicians have not been of the caliber to generate history on a level equal to that of the intrepid French and Spanish. Politics confined internally to Florida seems always to have sufficed the ambitions of Florida politicians; no one from state politics has ever fought the good fight all the way to national prominence. State politics was enough.

Denied any of the tradition, at least for effort if not for distinction that comes with success in national politics, Florida has consequently almost escaped the inevitable notoriety of political scandal that accompanies the spotlight of national prominence. The legacy of Osceola's betrayal might have forewarned of a frontier milieu where Mississippi Bubbles, Teapot Domes, and Yazoo Land schemes might occur. But only the disputed election returns of 1876, resulting in Rutherford B. Hayes' election as president over Samuel Tilden, muddy the otherwise politically bland color of the escutcheon of Florida's political past right down to the election of 2000. Bland is a hue in favor with politicians unwilling to risk the kind of innovative leadership that might result in failure. Bob Graham floated a brief balloon. Reuben Askew dreamed overnight of possibilities. So despite the near-misses in the careers of George Smathers, Claude Kirk, and LeRoy Collins, Florida has not enjoyed the furies of political power equal to the length of its history or, in recent times, its population.

Florida has become a very large population without acquiring the power that usually accompanies size. Since the 1990 census Florida has enjoyed the fourth largest electoral vote. In reaching fourth place between 1980 and 1990, Florida's population swept past Michigan, Illinois, Ohio, and Pennsylvania in the census, its nearest competitors during those years. But those four states have sent eight presidents, two vice presidents, four Senate floor leaders, seven speakers of the House, more than a dozen Supreme Court justices, and one hundred nineteen cabinet officers to Washington. In only the ten years between 1980 and 1990 during which Florida outgrew those four states, they realized Secretaries of State, Defense, Agriculture, Commerce, Transportation, and an Attorney General. Florida has not equaled the political elan of its recently surpassed rivals, as it looks now to the topmost tier of states still surpassing Florida's population, again states of long traditions of political activism.

In not developing as an aggressive political arena, Florida did not develop the corresponding tradition that comes with the exercise over many years of expanding and developing political machinery. Not admitted to the Union until 1845, Florida did not participate in the first fifteen national elections, from George Washington's first term to the aborted term of Zachary Taylor, during the years of some of the country's most enlightened and enduring political dialogue. Thus no Florida voice was heard in the writing of such seminal documents as the Constitution, the Federalist Papers, or any Supreme Court decision giving direction to American-style democracy. For its first seven elections after admission to statehood and the political process, from Franklin Pierce through U.S. Grant's first term, Florida had only the requisite minimum of three electoral votes. Today only seven states— Vermont, Delaware, South Dakota, Wyoming, Montana, North Dakota, and Alaska—still have only the minimum three electoral votes. Dade and Broward Counties have as much House representation as those seven states. The gay and lesbian Human Rights Campaign represent more people than those seven states. But small size does not seem to hamper other states. Maine, Vermont, and New Hampshire have had between them twenty national leaders, including three presidents, one vice president, two speakers of the House of Representatives, eleven cabinet officers, and three Justices of the Supreme Court. Florida has enjoyed none of that level of national prominence. Florida did not get its fifth electoral vote for another thirty years, when Theodore Roosevelt was elected in 1904. Florida advanced from five to six electoral votes during the next eight years, but then stalled in population till it got the seventh vote in 1932 with the next Roosevelt. Florida reached ten electoral votes only with the election of Eisenhower. So Florida has taken a long time growing to the size of a major political player among the states. That time should have been sufficient for the development of the skill needed to exert national levels of leadership. But Florida is now only populous, not powerful and influential. Florida's role, as that is determined by the careers of national leaders, is still essentially at the same level as when it entered the Union, except in Electoral College votes.

Today Florida is third among the fifty states in numbers of citizens, but far from third among major political players. The two larger states and the one more recently eclipsed for third largest population in the Union have enjoyed the political patronage flowing from eight presidents, fourteen vice presidents, twenty two Supreme Court justices, seven speakers of the House, and one hundred ten cabinet officers. Not even the present level of electoral support has been enough to convince any recent Florida leader to seek national leadership. There is no guarantee, of course, that a well-connected Floridian in the councils of power would necessarily help Florida develop not just military bases but the great institutions that are the hallmarks of the great states. But a home constituency in Florida to which the powerful would be answerable might help convince Floridians of Professor Tebeau's predictions. Assessing governors, Florida set a high-water mark in the 1950s with LeRoy Collins following Brown vs. Board of Education, an era of racial tension Collins navigated with distinction. But Virginia got Thomas Jefferson, New Jersey Woodrow Wilson, New York two Roosevelts, Even Georgia, next door, with not much to brag about theretofore, got Jimmy Carter. One of the four "big" states now, Florida has shown little inclination since getting into that square of the big-state corners of the U.S., to imitate the notable experience of California or New York, but instead more resembles the Texas model. With felons who've served their sentences, yet are penalized in perpetuity for political gain; with the state financed on the same tax on school supplies for billionaires as for working single moms; with the uninsured lacking affordable health care; with immigration policy that violates the great promise of the New World, the state government is simply not propelling Florida forward. Perhaps when Florida is both a big state and an old state, it will be a big state like California, or New York, not like Texas. If the absence of political dynamism had allowed the state to remain a backwater, a lack of suburban sprawl would have been worth the ignominy of political limbo. Can the oldest of places in the United States have so little impact on the course of affairs of state? If history counted for as much as politics, rather than being all too often the unfortunate consequence of politics, in some ideal world, Florida would lead the roll call of states. Professor Tebeau's prediction that Florida would play a greater role in national affairs might yet come to pass. But such a turn of events is still in the future. With twenty seven members of Congress today, no one holds in Florida's behalf a position of national consequence, neither Democrat nor Republican, equal to that of Mississippi, Georgia, Tennessee, and Arkansas in 1995, four states containing no more voters combined than Florida alone. Yet at mid-century only

Arkansas of those four was smaller than Florida, and those four states combined were five times bigger than the Florida of 1950. Florida today has obviously outgrown those four states combined more than once, but that growth is not reflected in any increase in potency in national affairs. Those four states have recently held among them the four most influential offices in national government.

Florida has not benefited from vigorous political leadership from its leaders or from all of its recently sizable citizenry. The first pioneers in Florida, Spanish priests and conquistadors, crowded into tiny wooden sailing ships and crossed stormy, unknown seas determined to find gold and adventure. Arriving to find only golden sunshine, of which there was already familiar abundance back home in Spain, they had the stamina and the wherewithal, albeit with a reputation for cruelty to the aboriginal population, to push on in quest of other objectives, sometimes less lofty, though all subsequent benefits of history derive directly from their insatiable curiosity to explore distant horizons. Today's pioneers are more apt to go tubing down the Ichetucknee, or to be retirees whose most burning ambitions drive them only to monitor the stock market, continue their basking, and complain of bugs. Their agenda is set by AARP more than by the needs of twenty-first century Florida. The leadership they have set in high place asks nothing that might disturb those made comfortable by a vibrant tourist economy. Florida was in the hands of more vigorous, adventurous leadership under Ponce de León, Hernando de Soto, Pánfilo de Narváez, Pedro Menéndez de Avilés, Jean Ribault, René de Laudonnière, or Osceola than it has been under any of its leaders in the modern era of American statehood. Historians of Florida today routinely traverse the annals of Florida's past all the way back across the entire twentieth century to Napoleon Bonaparte Broward, Governor from 1906 to 1910, in order to cite what they consider the apex of vigorous modern leadership in Florida, though Broward was a developer of the same kinds of commercial areas plaguing Florida now, and not a developer of great and lasting institutions. Andrew Jackson was Florida's first American governor, but the vain, intemperate Jackson left behind only geographical place names and a tradition of disdain for those who were the first Floridians. His bold if ruthless leadership has left no imprint of imaginativeness or willfulness recognizable in the mould in which Florida's leaders are generally cast. Florida's elected leadership has chosen to perpetuate itself by perpetrating the fallacy that an ever-expanding population proves that the leadership is doing its job well.

Now in the new millennium, only five years beyond the quincentennial Pascua Florida, Florida has been served the last by its good-old-boy he-coon son-of-Polk County citrus-ridge governors. Now, and perhaps for a long time hereafter, the governors of Florida will likely be more representative of newer Floridians, like the son of an ex-president, more familiar with the White House than with the statehouse, unable to decide whether his identity is Texan, Washingtonian, or favorite son of Kennebunkport, Maine. But it remains to be seen whether anything will change. The last Maine-born governor of Florida, Marcellus Lovejoy Stearns, having succeeded to that office just two years before the scandal of 1876, was thought to have been the last overt sign of Reconstruction in Florida. Florida has not garnered noticeably high marks for leadership at the national level with either its native born or its imported political officials. The expanding census of retirees has clearly marked the passage of years, but few of their political acts have moved Florida toward high distinction within the union.

It is admittedly difficult to feel much political motivation on sugary beaches, beneath rhythmically clacking palm fronds. Such places yield more readily to advertising than to politics. Consequently, Florida has been completely bypassed by the level of political maturity necessary to national governance. Socially, it often appears suspended between a child's playground sandbox and a nursing home, far from the corridors of political power or even from the social register, except the transitory one of "Mr. and Mrs..., of Boston and (sometimes) Palm Beach." The problem with that arrangement is that while the sales tax on their purchases goes to Tallahassee, political power still flows to places of developed political acumen, like Boston, or New York, or Los Angeles, and the legacies of their last will and testament go largely to institutions elsewhere, rather than to university, symphony, or museum endowments in Florida. Florida continues to be denied a role consonant with its position among the states as a very large state, third largest for the last ten years. Florida's large population has not occurred just within the last ten years, but has been in the making throughout much of this century. For its first half-century of statehood beginning in 1845, Florida enjoyed the benefits of the backwater, its vast natural areas undisturbed by burgeoning population. The second half-century saw the opening up of the peninsula to growing cities, as a consequence of the railroad builders at the turn of the century. During this last half-century Florida has exploded to a population of proportions far beyond the imagination of the state's elected officials for political guidance.

Florida deserves better as it basks in the five hundredth anniversary of the fabled first Pascua Florida, the sixth century of some kind of political life on these beautiful shores.

1995

10

The Culture of Tourism

It is symptomatic of the difficulty of developing the cultural milieu of Florida that the job of the office of Florida Secretary of State is the unlikely combination of elections and culture. It has now been a generation since many Secretaries of State could manage even accurate elections. Culture on no level has ever competed very successfully with politics for official encouragement, at least not since sixteenth-century art proved a more powerful propaganda weapon than munitions to the popes and kings of that era. And even Renaissance masters were ultimately subservient to the politics they served. Today only that art backed by capitalist titans on the scale of such collections as those of the Corcorans, Whitneys, Morgans, Mellons, Rockefellers, Guggenheims or Gettys is free from the indifferent if not hostile nature of politics or the marketplace.

Florida has benefited from only one such benefactor: John Ringling of circus fame and his extensive art collection and home, Ca d'Zan, as part of The John and Mable Ringling Museum of Art in Sarasota. If early developers such as the Plants, Flaglers, Disstons, and Chipleys had followed John Ringling's example, Florida might rival the most illustrious collections anywhere. Disney built a splendid symphony hall near their California resort, Disneyland. No similar contribution was made when Disney World opened in Florida in October, 1971.

Florida does have some notable collections of art: The Lowe, the Charles Hosmer Morse Tiffany collection, Cummer, Norton, Appleton, St. Petersburg Municipal, Ringling, Dali, among others—but only the Ringling has world-class architecture to house them. In contrast to Ringling, others built big houses but did not leave the great art treasures that filled them: Flagler's Whitehall, Rockefeller's The Casements, Deering's Vizcaya, F. C. Bartlett's Bonnet House, and Post's Mar-a-Lago. What might have been exemplary collections too frequently went north when estates were settled, along with large endowments to alma maters and museums. Georges Seurat's "Sunday Afternoon on the Island of La Grande Jatte," along with other works from Bartlett's collection by Picasso, Van Gogh, Matisse, and Gauguin did not stay in the Bonnet House in Ft. Lauderdale but instead went to Chicago. Most of those great collectors seemed to have remembered Florida primarily for its glorious winters, just like tin-can tourists. But the most influential of early Florida entrepreneurs did not collect and make available museums of world-class art open to the public. Instead, they built the hotels that ushered in the Florida of tourism.

Many important artists vacationed in Florida but came to paint weather, not history, or home. They did not establish artist's retreats, except for Martin Heade Johnson, who lived in St. Augustine and operated an art school from 1883 till his death in 1904, and the Maitland Center, in a delightful "Mayan-Art Deco" setting. Henry Flagler set an art colony in motion in St. Augustine, but it withered when he moved to grander quarters at Whitehall in Palm Beach. His railroad siphoned artists from St. Augustine to South Florida. Floridians today can be grateful for the Brown collection at Daytona's Museum of Arts and Sciences and especially the Vickers collection which is the largest anywhere of Florida scenes by prominent nineteenth-century artists like George Inness, William Morris Hunt, Winslow Homer, William Glackens and George Catlin.

The best American writers flocked to Key West in winter but seldom wrote of the experience, and established no Yaddo, or MacDowell, or anything less modest than those great writer colonies. Writers once wintered in St. Augustine, then in Sarasota, but did not immortalize the experience. They came for warm winter sunshine, like everyone else.

Appreciation of the highest forms of art has generally had to precede in order to foster interest in less glamorous forms of art such as folk and primitive, and especially the aboriginal forms of art. The presence in Florida of collections of the most famous art of the world and the people who take an interest in it could have heightened interest in preserving the state's aboriginal past as well as helping to underwrite its cultural future. But without a long tradition of valuing and promoting serious art, few artifacts of Florida's aboriginal past have survived. Many burial mounds and kitchen middens were lost to development. The early Indians favored the same seashore sights as modern tourists. Thousands of years of the past were used by the state itself as filler for roadbeds, all ground into an unreclaimable pulverized roadbed filler on which to pour steaming asphalt.

The uses of the past might not have been lost had Florida evolved more quickly into an established society of big cities with distinguished old families with the means to indulge in art before the state became a popular playground. Much of Florida's evolutionary past disappeared only sixty or more years ago, before the enormous population growth of the 1960s and since made most recovery of the ancient past remote. Only a small fraction of the Weeden Island culture, the Fort Walton culture, or the Everglades culture have survived to be showcased, scarcely enough to allow any more than painfully fragmentary educated guesses about the native cultures of Florida. The aborigines themselves disappeared by about 1763. Traces of their past disappeared when Florida rushed virtually overnight from a sparsely populated, largely undeveloped poor state into the beginnings of one of the mega-states of America, but one not served by vast museums of the best art or the artistic traditions that make them possible.

However impressive the aboriginal Florida art that survives, like primitive art or art in general its impact on modern society has been limited by the pervasiveness of electronic popular culture. Even museums of the great art of Europe's most aesthetically vibrant eras find it difficult to compete for modern America's attention with the exponentially expanding juggernaut of professional sports, Hollywood, recording studios, and television. Florida's aboriginal past would perhaps offer stronger lessons if it at least were all housed in one place, rather than scattered among sites as disparate and remote from each other as the Silver River Museum (Ocala), the Bureau of Archaeological Research (Tallahassee), the Florida Museum of Natural History (Gainesville), the Temple Mound Museum (Fort Walton Beach), the Department of Anthropology, Florida Atlantic University (Boca Raton), the Graves Museum of Archaeology and Natural History (Dania), the University of Pennsylvania Museum (Philadelphia), the Museum of the American Indian (Washington), the Historical Society of Palm Beach County, Rollins College (Winter Park), the Fort Caroline National Memorial (Jacksonville), Tomoka State Park (Ormond Beach), the Historical Museum of Southern Florida (Miami), Princeton University (New Jersey), the Jacksonville Museum of History and Science, the South Florida Museum and Bishop Planetarium (Bradenton), the Smithsonian Institution (Washington), and numerous private collections. Admirably brought together in Barbara A. Purdy's 1996 *Indian Art of Ancient Florida* (Gainesville: University Presses of Florida), the art of aboriginal Florida suggests above all else the response of a people to their environment, a lesson made imperative by the growth in population in Florida.

Florida's environment cannot withstand the vigor of modern civilization the way less fragile, more naturally stable topography can. Both art and the landscape it springs from would gain from the relationship between the two expressed by the earliest art forms. The environment of Florida would be less at risk if the composer Frederick Delius had fostered another Salzburg, Glyndebourne, or Bayreuth on the St. Johns he lived beside, drawing musicians in search of inspiration to the cacophony of wilderness Florida. It is unfortunate that Zephaniah Kingsley's Whistler connections, his sister having become the grandmother of James McNeill Whistler, did not metamorphose into a St. Johns Valley School of landscape painters the equal of the Hudson River Valley School. A gallery such as the Vickers Collection of masterpieces of scenes of the St. Johns helps assert public recognition of that river today. There is the Vickers art and Frederick Delius's music of the St. Johns. But what Florida especially has is the St. Johns itself. Stephen Foster might have inspired another Nashville, or Motown, on the Suwannee. But Florida's legacy is, instead, the Suwannee itself. It is a unique landscape, its own form of art, and since it cannot be protected within museum walls, it has to be honored for the treasure it is. There are many jewels of natural Florida preserved: numerous springs flowing into ink-black rivers, beach coasts and marsh coasts, and parks like the Marie Selby, Sunken Gardens, Maclay Gardens, Washington Oaks, Cypress Gardens, McKee Gardens, Fairchild Gardens, Ravine Gardens, the Morikami and more, plus two hundred state parks and forests, but too often they remind one of great swaths of Florida lost to development.

In 1900 Florida had fewer than one million people. Salvage crews had made Key West the largest city in the state. St. Augustine was second, Tallahassee, third. During those years, today's tiny Apalachicola was the largest port and cotton-shipping commercial center in Florida. Today, US1, A1A, I95, and the Florida Turnpike run side-by-side through the great populations from Palm Beach to Miami, none of them scarcely five miles from the Atlantic, strung together like guitar strings. Everyone wants to be on a beach. So did the Tequesta. The sea was where they found their greatest supply of food, the same beach where we only sunbathe. Had there been a Peabody Museum, founded in 1866, or a Penn Museum of Archaeology and Anthropology, founded in 1887, or a Chicago Oriental Institute, founded in 1919, in Florida, investigating the mounds and middens lining those shores, road builders would not likely have been able to use those sites as road filler. Florida would celebrate ample evidence of one of the oldest histories in the New World. The job of preserving the aboriginal culture of Florida would have been easier in that generation. Even as late as World War II, Florida was the smallest of the Southern states. South Carolina, Arkansas, Mississippi each had more citizens than Florida. But hardly a single decade into the post-war economic boom passed before Florida mushroomed into a state with two million people. It is a simple matter now to discern that just as tourists had poured into Florida on the railroad cars at the beginning of the twentieth century, so even more would pour into Florida if an adequate highway system were developed. And when the highways were developed, the people came.

Florida had not developed at the beginning of the century because it was too sparsely populated with an educated citizenry and was too poor. It did not develop very quickly even at mid-century because it was too busy keeping up with the massive numbers of vacationers the state itself had lured. When Florida prepared in 1964 to celebrate the quadricentennial of St. Augustine's founding with the reprinting by the University Press of Florida of significant early Florida histories and travel guides, the state took as its justifying text that Florida had "entered the select circle of the ten most populous states of the nation," and while "Neither number nor age is necessarily a distinction,...most Americans are impressed by the former and revere the latter." But the reprinting of copies of Florida's most ancient history texts did not create momentum leading to cultural development commensurate with the eagerly-sought growth in population. Despite the absence of a museum with the resources of the visiting Rockefellers, Flaglers, Plants and Bonnets, or the library left behind by visiting writers like Tennessee Williams, Wallace Stevens, Thornton Wilder and Sinclair Lewis, among others, Florida is dotted with small, notable, exotic treasures more distinctively Florida than Disney World. A partial list includes: one of the ten Karpeles manuscript museums, the A. E. Backus museum of his Florida canvases, the Florida Highwaymen artists, the Museum of Florida's Art and Culture, the Asolo Theater, the twelfth-century Spanish monastery of St. Bernard of Clairvaux, the home of Frederick Delius, the home of Harriet Beecher Stowe, the Stranahan house, Bok Tower, the Ponce de León and Tampa Bay hotels, the home of Carlisle Floyd, the grave of Randolph Caldecott, Cross Creek, the Barnacle, Laura Riding Jackson's last home, and Alice Walker's headstone on Zora Neale Hurston's previously unmarked pauper's grave. And beyond the actual, for the truly imaginative there is William Bartram's description of the clear Santa Fe River disappearing underground, then reappearing in Samuel Taylor Coleridge's "Kubla Khan," the open sea off Daytona Beach where Stephen Crane was on board a ship sailing from Jacksonville to Cuba to report on the Spanish-American war when the ship sank and Crane narrowly made it to shore in "The Open Boat," or the beach where Ponce de León stepped ashore in 1513 thus commencing historic Florida. Florida's appeal was, after the passing of the illusion of gold five hundred years ago, still its exotic landscape, now filled with cultural and natural treasure, exotic and unexpected. Yet none of these sites have the gravitas to draw tourists away from the spell of Disney World. The Everglades is too fragile to distract the average tourist from the behemoth that is Disney World. Miami's stunning skyline is just housing. Hopefully, Art Basel Miami Beach will be the masterpiece that beckons to those million-plus tourists something more befitting the glory that is Florida.

Florida was a state in which there was for a long time minimal establishment of the agents of curatorial authority over the artifacts of the cultural past, without which there was little inducement to preserve natural Florida. Early modern Florida has been rescued by the Florida Trust for Historic Preservation. There were no large and powerfully active university departments of archaeology and anthropology, no heavily endowed museums with departments of aboriginal antiquity, no historians molding evocative images of the past, no rich and influential philanthropic foundations attuned to the aboriginal past. Though Florida had been the arena of builders whose financial clout was the equal of the Rockefellers, the Morgans, or the Mellons, those builders drawn to Florida did not do here what their counterparts had done in the established cities of the northeast. Flagler and Plant built railroads and hotels, not art museums and libraries of antiquities. Since their time, the later Balls, duPonts, Lykes, or Fanjuls have not been interested in making haute culture public in Florida. Florida should by right of location in the subtropics have been home to the greatest gardens since Babylon. Dr. Henry Perrine began such an effort before Florida was a state but was killed in the Seminole Wars. Later, the work of David Fairchild began again the same cultural effort. But his effort had been limited by the amount of effort required simply to maintain against an exploding population what he had begun, rather than expanding into one of the natural wonders of the world.

So there was for a long time in Florida insufficient consciousness of the worth of primitive art and the nature that inspired it to explore and preserve what remained. The aboriginal past is typically the last to come to the attention of the forces of education, culture, and government which might preserve it. Perhaps because of the European basis of western education, the art of an era of history perceived as the most enlightened gets first attention. The British took note of their famous Roman past long before attending to their much more linguistically and racially important but less well received Anglo-Saxon or Celtic past. Neither fields of prehistoric plinth nor caves at Lascaux were for many generations celebrated in France with the attention given to Gothic cathedrals and stained-glass windows. Had Calusan, Tequestan, and Timucuan village sites, middens, as well as other artifacts been not the aboriginal past, but rather remains of Roman forts, road, walls and aqueducts, they would even in early Florida more likely have been preserved, and thus contributed to the cultural milieu throughout the state on every level. Had they been the work of the pharaohs who built the pyramids, they would have been preserved. Had they been the everlasting stone remains of medieval cathedrals and monasteries, they would have been protected. If the Spanish, victims of a diabolical La Leyenda Negra, abetted by academia and nationalistic Protestantism, had not been followed by mercantil-

istic English-Americans, more of the earliest history of Florida would likely have been saved. Florida's primitive aboriginal
tribes are unlike other native tribes as the ancestors of no one
living today, especially of any group in economic or political
power or of Native American cultures which have finally begun to achieve cachet. They have not been automatically included in widely used texts and thus made easily familiar, and
so traces of them have not acquired the image of other more
popular western Native American groups. Without the drawings of Jacques Le Moyne, the diaries of a few early explorers,
and a scant roomful of wood, bone, clay and metal artwork
they would have disappeared entirely.

Florida has been too transfixed by the effort to get others to enjoy the beaches to turn attention to the Florida that
has long been here. That is the unglamorous, costly, and very
time-consuming process of the historian, the archaeologist,
the novelist, the enlightened citizen, and the responsible jour-
nalist working a lifetime with little notice, which sometimes
would not come even in a lifetime. Having drifted from 1513
until 1925, Florida has not for the last very busy ninety-five
years been the kind of state to wait on the continued slow
process of time. Since the boom era of the 1920s Florida's
pace has been an almost officially adopted state policy of fre-
neticism to get the state developed and to get it full of people.
That was throughout the last century the almost single hallmark with which the guiding hand in Florida has led the way.
Fortunately, Windover, the Miami Circle, San Luis Apalachee
and other sites suggest a growing commitment to the legacy
of the past. Tourism can be a vital addition to an economy,
and a motivation to keep an area easily accessible and widely
celebrated. But it seems to be less deleterious to the environ-

ment if an attraction is not built for the purpose of luring tourists, especially by today's standards of size. Disney World and Las Vegas are immeasurably vast beyond yesterday's Marineland, Silver Springs, or Sunken Gardens. More care is taken when a site draws tourists because of its natural beauty (Grand Canyon, Blue Ridge Parkway) or because of historical significance (Stonehenge, Teotihuacan, Castillo de San Marco).

When Florida began noticeably to take the lead among states in growth at mid-century, the excitement was such that no effort by builders of institutions engaged in art or archaeology could possibly have had equal time in the press or in legislative councils with accounts of swelling populations in south Florida. Now Florida is third among the states in size of population, playing in a cultural league hitherto unfamiliar to the office of Secretary of State. Its competitors at the top are California, New York, and Texas, home to some of the most notable institutions in the nation, though those states did not necessarily need their head start over Florida. Florida was unprepared to match the efforts even of its Southern neighbors. Georgia built the first public college to be chartered in America, in 1785, three years before it became one of the first thirteen states of the new union. Its neighbor, North Carolina, was a close second in 1789, in its first year of statehood. Tennessee recognized the priority of education before the turn of the eighteenth century, establishing the University of Tennessee in 1794, two years before achieving statehood. South Carolina began a state college in 1801, Virginia in 1819, Alabama in 1820, its second year of statehood. Even Mississippi created the beginnings of a university in 1844, a full decade before Florida began to organize a system of public higher education in 1851. In fairness, the rudiments of a university in Florida were chartered only ten years after Florida's admission to statehood. But it had not only the example of its sister southern states but had already been organized as a territory of the United States for twenty-five years. The same slowness in Florida to organize has also been true in private education. Methodist and Presbyterian pioneers elsewhere in the rest of the South did not rush to Florida to rescue it from its historic Catholic beginnings. William and Mary was chartered in Virginia in 1693, the College of Charleston in 1770. Duke, Tulane, Emory and Davidson came along in the 1830s, Birmingham-Southern and Sewanee in the 1850s. Private education did not begin in Florida until Rollins, Stetson, and Florida Southern were chartered in the 1880s.

Outside established metropolitan areas there is often little else but the nearest college attempting to foster a cultural milieu. In Tennessee, the nation's oldest collegiate literary quarterly, *The Sewanee Review*, began publishing in 1892, forty years after Florida organized its first college. Florida still does not have a literary quarterly the equal of *The Virginia Quarterly Review*, begun in 1925, or *The Southern Review*, begun at Louisiana State University in 1935. Though without a long tradition of literary quarterlies, however, Florida has fared better with historiography. *The Florida Historical Quarterly*, published since 1908, is the publishing agency of the Florida Historical Society, formed in 1856. The distinguished senior publication has inspired several younger historical periodicals, such as *Tequesta*, *Apalachee*, *Tampa Bay History*, *Spanish River Papers*, *El Escribano* and others. The University Press of Florida is especially notable for efforts to make the publications of the earliest

Florida history available. But had Florida government encouraged broadly significant traditions and means of scholarly inquiry into history and archaeology before making the highways equal in importance to the health, education, and welfare of its citizens, all aspects of Florida could be celebrated today with more understanding.

It is now too late to acquire a vastly more extensive knowledge than already exists of the lost Calusan, Tequestan, Timucuan past. But it is not too late to recognize the importance of those first Floridians. Lacking long traditions in other forms of the arts, Florida is dependent on archaeology and the earliest cultural forms. For the lost tribes, Florida owes the Calusans, Timucuans, Tequestans, Aiis, Jeagas and Apalachees an expression of consciousness, if not apology. Canada is able to apologize to aboriginals there. If political correctness did not appropriate useful phrases of language, what Anglo-Saxons did to the original Floridians would be called a crime against humanity. Instead, any historian's slight reference usually comes in the form of wistful footnotes. It is not too late to reclaim remnants of later chapters in Florida history still reservable, helping to focus attention on the extraordinary reach of Florida history. Their likeness has been lost, except for the drawings of Le Moyne. If we knew the appearance of them, as George Catlin's portrait made possible with Osceola, there might now be a Calusa County, or Tequestatown, or Jeagaville.

There might perhaps be, in an effort to reclaim a sense of the past, yet another rotunda of notables of those likenesses not lost even if sadly neglected. Perhaps the old capitol in Tallahassee is the most suitable for a place of honor reserved exclusively for those who created Florida, honoring the long line-up of individuals, both charlatans and heroes, before the English and the capitalist entrepreneurs, who have contributed in important ways to the most fabulous history of any of the states: not just the obligatory Ponce de León and Hernando de Soto, but the love story of Ucita and Ulalah and Juan Ortiz, the wanderer Cabeza de Vaca, Pedro Menéndez de Avilés, Osceola, Jean Ribaut, Pánfilo de Narváez, Vincente Martinez Ybor, Luis Cáncer de Barbastro, Hernando de Escalante Fontaneda, Estéban, René de Laudonnière, Tristán de Luna, Dominic de Gourgues, Coacoochee, Alonso Escobedo, José Martí, Bishop Calderon, Martin Prieto and Baltasar Lopez, Francisco Pareja, Neamathla, Bernard Romans, Jacques le Moyne, Don Andrés de Arriola, Bernard Galvez and, of course, others innumerable even for a grateful, cognizant public. It is difficult to say where such a list of names vital to early Florida, each as vital in his or her own way as another, or as Carlos of the Calusas or Saturiba of the Timucuans, chiefs when the Spanish first arrived, might end before a balance were struck with the coming generations of all-encompassing English-surnamed Floridians.

Memory would be served by a second rotunda next door to that French, Native American, and Spanish first one, for those with English names who though later in time are just as indispensable to Florida's past, the men and women responsible for all the myth and legend as much as the military and political personalities history always carefully records: Zephaniah Kingsley, William Chipley, Alexander McGillivray, Jonathan Gibbs, Mary Grace Quackenbos, Addison Mizner, Richard Campbell, Mark Catesby, Andrew Turnbull, Robert Ranson, Woodbury Lowery, Susan Eppes, David Levy Yulee, Buckingham Smith, Colonel Titus, William Augustus Bowles,

Minnie Moore Wilson, John Ringling, even Plant and Flagler. We do as much for governors who often did less. Elected government unfailingly honors its own, most of whom would be virtually unknown except for the offices they were elevated to. This would be for those who made Florida without benefit necessarily of elective office.

It is by any reasonable scenario time now for the leadership of Florida to cease from further celebration of the extraordinary population of this new old state. It is not the time to wonder when national football championships will balance out in number among teams in Miami, Gainesville, and Tallahassee, or soon, Orlando and Tampa. It is time for the leadership to ask why the largest number of Nobel laureates in teaching is gathered at a public institution in California, rather than Florida; why the largest endowment of any public college in the world is in Texas, not Florida; why the greatest municipal library in the world is in New York and not in Florida. These are the playing fields on which a competition might be won that would result in the recognition of Florida as third among the fifty. Population alone is hardly the key to distinction. Many political entities across the globe are larger than Florida without the same promise of distinction. The Ted Turner or Bill Gates of our time excepted, neither of them Floridians anyway, the time is quite obviously past when individuals alone could provide the costly distinction made available by the patrons of the past. The only entity in Florida that can make of this the third among the states of the union is the state itself. Government is the problem only to those who have not tried actually to visit in person every single one of Florida's state parks and forests. Luckily, Florida has a matchless system of state parks, though supported inconsistently.

It is of course too late in the history of the world to expect to develop standard institutions of culture that could compete on even terms with the world's greatest museums, the libraries of rare manuscripts and incunabula, or the most impressive collections of dinosaur fossils. That seemed recently to be the province exclusively of the Japanese. The truly rich of our time make the effort to win back time only where the public is willing to spend enormous amounts in order to establish instant professional sports traditions. It is almost too late to enshrine the only treasure that makes Florida distinctive in world geography, the only resource it has that could make it the equal of its imagined competition in the other colossal States of the American Union, and that is its natural beauty, unlike any natural wonder anywhere in the world. But if Florida is ever to be synonymous with its competition as a leader in any version of distinctively American culture, the preservation of the most pristine, the most original Florida, and not merely an increased population, or the celebration of sunshine, is Florida's challenge.

2014

11

Trails to Pascua 600

A visitor driving down the length of Florida on Interstate 75 or the Sunshine State Parkway might easily imagine at work there the uninterrupted genius of the Roman Empire for roadbuilding. From the highway, Florida gives every evidence that it must be among the most professionally administered states in the union. Florida builds first-class highways. Road signs are professionally designed and maintained. Shoulders are planted and trimmed. Rest-stops are mercifully frequent, modern, clean, and secure; moreover, driving down the exit ramp off the highway on to surface roads and streets the visiting driver is in the hands of the tourist economy geared to meet the transient's desire for first-class levels of convenience. Parking spaces surround every building. The visiting driver is in a world with apparently no thought but his driving and parking ease. In the midst of the only geography to offer not one but two magnificent coasts just miles from each other, Florida's highways allow even the most casual of visitors to indulge in a frenzied flitting heliotropically back and forth from Atlantic to Gulf.

The highway culture does not end with the highways themselves, either, in Florida. Any traveler who has dealt with any variety of state police elsewhere likely recognizes that the Florida Highway Patrol is a highly professional organization. Any driver who has ever relocated to a new home elsewhere in the South as well as to Florida and applied for a driving license in both states knows how professionally Florida administers a program that elsewhere is all too often a nightmare of inefficiency. So about highways and the experience of driving, Florida puts its best foot to the pedal.

But for those who remain here to make a life, whose needs are not reflected only in those conveniences so admired by the tourist, official Florida is less perspicacious. It is unarguable that as individuals we have willingly mortgaged everything to the driver and his automobile, whether he is tourist or resident. It can even be argued that having met the needs of the driver, the state has met the needs regarded as paramount by the majority of the citizens any of the United States. And that is probably true. But it is indefensible for the highest levels of state policy to operate, to legislate and budget, in such a fashion that the state actually believes the needs of the driver to be his paramount need as a citizen, to attend to that need above so many other needs of the people of Florida.

When the paving of Florida can finally be reviewed objectively, equally with all the other needs of a citizenry, the state will claim that it did only what the voters wanted, and that, too, is unfortunately true. But it cannot be called leadership. For the state to pave all Florida because it pacifies voters and visitors is closer to campaigning than governing, especially not a level of governance that actually leads. Roadbuilding is not statecraft, but politics, dispensing monies for the showiest rather than the neediest, sometimes least popular needs. Despite its ranking in even one area—size of population—among the three states in the top tier of states in the union, official Florida is ill-equipped by policy or inclusion to compete except for first place as a tourist destination. Of all the needs of its citizens, the state assumes full responsibility only for roads and, before vouchers, schools. The chronology of the state's acceptance of those two responsibilities says much about even those obligations. The Department of Road Building was created by a bill enacted in 1915. Compulsory school attendance did not begin until 1919. Free textbooks were not mandated until 1925. And the state draws distinctions between those two needs it selected at the beginning of the last century, maintaining quality state roads in every county, leaving some of the lesser ones to the county to build and maintain. The state does not maintain schools in every district, but leaves the matter of the quality of schools entirely up to the counties. There are no state schools and county schools competing for attention in each school district, as there are roads. If in the American mythology of provincial responsibility schools are too important to be turned over to the centralized state authority but must be run locally, surely roads are less important ultimately than schools.

The state does not insist on hospitals, parks, libraries, museums, or even grocery stores and pharmacies, telephones, electricity, indoor plumbing, or police and fire protection in whatever remote corner of the state the citizen may choose to homestead. But it does take on that role in the area of roads and schools. And therein lies the problem; by declaring those two needs paramount, two vastly different projects become the hallmarks of government responsibility, one virtually impossible to measure, the other painfully obvious to measure. Naturally, government has done its best by the project easiest to measure. Any fool knows good roads from bad, but no one really knows the quality of a school. Florida focuses on roadbuilding as the primary need of all its citizens, as though there were still destinations of irresistible desirability and accessible by road, just as the federal Congress focuses on armaments building as though there were still evil empires besieging the nation's gates.

As it is the obligation of the United States to "form a more perfect Union," it should be the obligation of official Florida to promote a more perfect state. But the state's obligation in fulfilling such an ambition goes beyond good highways. It goes, as well, beyond schools. In order to ensure a more perfect state, it seems necessary for the state to be able to see beyond the absolutely most obvious assets possible in the very visible form of miles of asphalt and citizens with cars to drive on them. It will require more of the state than to permit Disney's advertising budget to create the illusion that Florida is well governed in all areas of government responsibility because it is so appealing to so many people as a place to wile away empty hours. The state panders to popular culture when it abandons the public to its own levels of diversion. It is far more difficult and costly to encourage the coalitions that can provide the benefits of serious forms of haute culture that result in high mindedness. The state would not in good conscience abandon its children to their own desires, but encourages high mindedness through free compulsory education.

Florida cannot, of course, right all wrongs. No country on the globe has succeeded in eliminating poverty, sickness, racism, ignorance, and injustice, or in forming a perfect union. Some problems are less remediable than others. No legislation will make Florida the dreamland of the geologist as it is the hydrologist. But Florida is not well served by so steady a focus on highways as to obscure those aspects of good governance that require more imagination to remediate. The outrage of transportation as the supreme need should have reached its apogee with the spanning of the Florida Keys by rail. But the incessant pandering to roads now offers a highway whereby one can drive an automobile over one hundred miles of open sea. Key West once managed to become and remain, for most of the century, the largest city in Florida without benefit of highways, railroads, or even wagon trails. If Key West were accessible today only by boat or train, it would still be the island paradise it was from the first Pascua until tawdry tourism replaced the charm of island living. Yet Florida, despite good systems of state parks and forest, a professionally administered wildlife and marine fisheries, as well as other indications of a sincere desire to govern for the ages, nevertheless continues to focus on roadbuilding as though it were 1930 and roads were still the primary means of addressing the ideal state.

The twentieth century began in Florida with a boom in highways construction. And it was a good century in which Florida has righted many wrongs. In 1900 Florida still had no prison systems but leased prisoners to be slaves in work camps run by private individuals empowered to determine punishment for infractions. Free compulsory public primary or secondary education did not exist. But now the century is over and we are a generation past the five hundredth Pascua Florida. The danger now is not that there might still be some crevice of Florida still not served by paved public roads. The danger now is that we will pave, pollute, and overpopulate the Panhandle and Peninsula out of any of the historical and natural appeal that has drawn the non-indigenous newcomer since 1513.

For the century to have ended the same way it began suggests little progress from what was then frontier Florida up to third among players in the union. Instead of singling out roads and schools as the only statewide needs, why was there never the same system of a Board of Commissioners in every community in charge of building libraries, museums, art galleries, parks and music clubs, among amenities satisfying civilization, within easy reach of every citizen in the state, an obligation of government to be undertaken by the state just as road building is? This commission, made up of members representing each congressional district, funded by dedicated taxes, would politic just as assiduously as road commissioners, competing for appointment to their jobs by making large donations to the winning candidates for high office, all in order to bring cultural largeness to their communities, as they have brought roads now for all the generations of the twentieth century. That roads are the only inviolable infrastructure is an idea that should have expired with the last century.

At the end of the nineteenth century the governors of Florida, following accepted prevailing political-economic pressures, gave away millions of acres of Florida to railroad builders, confident that Americans would always ride by rails.

Today, with almost no visitor dependent on railroads, Florida builds highways as though that would, ineluctably, always be the one sure route to a more perfect Florida. Future generations may travel in ways as yet unknown to roadbuilders relying on needs of the 1930s, brought to bear not by examining every possible requirement for good government but by Henry Ford. Surely priorities and the policies to secure them exist to lead to more equable and lasting benefits to Floridians than already provided virtually free by the climate. Having been given the gift of the world's most salubrious climate, it is especially incumbent on the state to address means in keeping with Florida's imagined position among the states. Neither highways nor one hundred million visitors traveling them make Florida third among players. Florida's twenty million residents can. A generation past the quincentennial Pascua Florida is surely the right time to reconsider what measures will advance Florida toward distinction.

The ascendance of Florida's image as a playground, subsuming the image of its politics, history, literature, and of its Southern and European heritages, can be remedied by a state capable of building such a remarkable network of highways and making world-famous the beaches they lead to. With the state virtually paved, the same energy and money that effort required could burnish the image of the more permanent and lasting Florida. If it is late to distinguish Florida by establishing the equal of the New York City Public Library, the university system of California, the Philadelphia Symphony, the San Diego Zoo, the Boston Museum of Fine Arts, or the Brooklyn Botanical Garden, it is not too late for Florida to find a way to achieve distinction through myriad means still at hand.

The distinction to which Florida might aspire need not be as glitteringly obvious as those great institutions. Though Florida has vast cattle ranching, citrus production, and truck farming, it has from the beginning of its cities in 1565, been organized less as an agrarian society and more as an urbanized society. Though despite a basically urban beginning, Florida has not experienced the advantage of great cities as they have evolved elsewhere. Unlike most of the world, in Florida the best museums, libraries, and similar cultural institutions that foster overall cultural awareness have evolved in some of the smallest cities of the state, dependent on the state government focused on highway building, rather than in large cities where wealthy patrons, rather than the state, support them. New York City did not build the Metropolitan or the philharmonic there; they are the legacies of generations of wealthy lovers of the arts helping to build the cities they lived in. Even the Smithsonian and the Library of Congress grew from collections of individuals. But modern economics are less likely to allow philanthropic individuals to accomplish what the state is fully capable of doing. Simply filling in wetlands in order to allow more people to crowd into the suburbs does not make a great city, except in the off chance that among those in the crowd will be a painter, a writer, musician, poet, naturalist, scientist or wealthy patron of the arts, someone, in short, who will become a student of that area, someone who will join his memory of his own past with his place in Florida and create from that combination images that will bring distinction to Florida themes.

That outcome is more likely to occur provided the kinds of facilities beyond paved roads, and even the sewer hookups or power lines that follow them, the kinds of facilities of the mind and spirit that will draw people to the towns and cities of Florida, where they will be encouraged to contribute beyond depositing Social Security checks. Florida deserves a *Miamian*, or *Tampan*, equal to the *New Yorker*. Florida public television deserves to equal the quality of WGBH in Boston. Florida should have a newspaper the equal of the *New York Times*. Newspapers have been published here since the St. Augustine *Gazette* announced England's defeat at the hands of George Washington in 1787. Florida deserves—dare one dream?—a Florida Broadcasting Corporation as honored for worthiness as the BBC.

Florida cannot afford to wait endlessly to acquire the quality of statehood it is destined for, and deserves. Sufficient experience is on hand at the approach of two hundred years of statecraft, five hundred years of tempering European models of city building. If one were to dream of the Florida that might come to pass with the coming of her sixth century of effort toward recorded civilization, it would begin with leadership able to focus on more than getting elected and, once elected, to be willing to make choices aimed at a posterity beyond the next election cycle. Instead, unafraid of the upcoming election, installed in high office at this moment, it would need to be a leadership willing to try to imagine the Florida waiting to be discovered by the Ponce de León of all our best hopes for a landscape unlike any other. The tourists of this millennium could find a Florida so ravishingly tended as to make it safe even from litter, let alone pollution.

Beyond whatever election season comes next, Florida could be a state capable of balancing a justly prized individualism with the now-elusive commonwealth. The effort to establish the right of the individual has been the hallmark of

American civilization. But an even more difficult challenge remains, and that is to encourage free individuals to put goals of the common good first. It may be enough for the individual to ask only that the road be there when he decides to travel, that an adequate school be nearby for his children. But the state must require more of itself and of its individuals.

The dream of the Florida to come might begin with the idealistic fantasy of the state budget for transportation divided into equal fourths for travel by rail, by water, and by air, as well as one fourth devoted to travel by automobile. The dream might include zoning that does not allow disfiguring ribbon-like towns and cities. In this dream, instruction in history, math, or language would be worth as much as coaching—kindergarten teaching would be valued at the same rate as graduate-school teaching. The dream includes a recycling effort sufficient to require no further elimination of raw materials. It leaves the natural beauty of Florida unmarred by placing unsightly power lines underground, or by not placing highways laid out on the very edge of the sea. It includes an educational program in the state parks budget equal to the amount spent to lure visitors to privately owned theme parks. After so much effort to build highways to bring the world to the beach, it would provide for a gas tax able to fund free university tuition, medical care, park and museum entrance rather than funding yet more highways. The dream offers a shoreline that would bring the hosannas of Pascua Florida to the lips of the Ponce de Leóns to come.

A generation or more of historians have observed that the twentieth century was the greatest watershed of all the eras of human history. From the dawn of history to the dawn of the twentieth century, the fastest mode of transportation known to man was a fresh rider on a fresh horse riding over level ground. The widest audience ever known to man was the number of people within the sound of the unamplified human voice. As the twenty-first century accumulates, by way of contrast, it is difficult to maintain daily record of human achievement. If the human species is to be cloned, the resulting numbers of us to be linked in cyberspace, it is especially difficult to guess how radically changed human activity may become.

But that is exactly the climate required to encourage leadership to reach for the very loftiest of goals for the future. The coming millennium will accelerate an already dizzying pace. Constantly updated news is available on events in the remotest corners of the globe now. It is difficult to sort out the really important news from the ephemeral. Chroniclers will look back increasingly wistfully to the keepers of the seventh- and eighth-century *Anglo-Saxon Chronicle*, the big book of annals rotating from monastery to monastery for recording ancient England's one big event of the year: "AD 679 In this year Aelfwine was slain, and St. Aethelthryth passed away"; "734 In this year the moon was as if it were suffused with blood; and Tatwine and Bede passed away." They recorded only the memorable, only the lastingly important. If the twenty-first century proves to be as challenging to account for on a daily basis as now seems accurately predictable, it will be even more challenging to recognize what really counts.

The outset of the last century first brought America's political prominence to a naturalist, when Theodore Roosevelt was elected president. But even so studiedly enthusiastic a naturalist as Roosevelt did not succeed in establishing equal prominence for craggy mountain peaks as well as ephemerally fragile wetlands. We still failed to measure adequately the difference between the two landscapes. But marsh is what has been vouchsafed to Florida. The recent Pascua is a good time to see the marsh and the history that has taken place there with a new perspective. Long-established measurements of value will remain true but will likely be even more elusive in the next century than in this. The pen, for example, will still be mightier than the sword. The human condition will still ordain our lot to be the passage from birth through suffering to death. Government policy will still be man's worst enemy, while government power will still be the only resource sufficient to provide and protect what is valuable. The beaches are gone to highrises. The marshes are going. Florida's leadership exchanged the nation's longest and most beautiful coastline, our single most glamorous asset, for a few cents sales tax income on the dollar. Every inch of Florida is at risk. Florida grows too fast to take its time in deciding what is most valuable long beyond the quincentenary Pascua. Florida's endowment is history and water. Both have been mortgaged. What might it require of this century to make Florida's image equal Florida's promise?

1998

12

Entering Sumter County

The big green sign on the side of Interstate 75 through Central Florida reads: "Entering Sumter County." Years ago, in a pre-interstate era, that county-line marker read "Enter Sumter County/Leave Marion County." It seems sadly appropriate to the current idiom of today's hurry-up Florida to use the participial, "Entering," rather than the imperative "Enter" used there when I was a boy and Florida had fewer than a million people. A driver across Florida then knew—was reminded, if he had forgotten—which county he had been driving through, where he had been, just as he was leaving.

Today the Interstates glide ceaselessly, seamlessly through flat Florida, marking only upcoming exits, the occasional state park. It is as if it doesn't matter any more what county one is in presently, for all of us will doubtless soon be in a different county, well before we've come to know enough about the one we're in to want to know why they called it Sumter, or Marion.

The Sumter-Marion County line marked the end of home for me throughout my first eighteen years. It was all I knew of the world. Because my grandmother, my daddy's mother, knew all about history and told it all to us, I knew early about Thomas Sumter the Gamecock, and Francis Marion the Swampfox, both South Carolina heroes of the American Revolution. Both counties had already been named by the time my ancestors migrated from Lancaster County, South Carolina, to Alachua County, Florida, in 1842, then on here to Sumter County in 1853. Did my folks way back then deliberately choose a new home in this Florida county because it had been named for their fellow South Carolinian? Would my ancestors have cared? No one in my family cares now. No one of them even knows why it is called what it is. My grandmother cared, when she lived here, but she has now been dead a generation. Was political lore, the romance of geographical place names, as blasé to my earliest ancestors here, 150 years ago, as it is to my family today?

Interest in Florida now runs to tourism, not history. We may know that Florida has the longest coastline of the forty-eight contiguous states, the whitest sand beaches, the longest north-flowing river, but we little celebrate its possession of so much lore—of Ponce de León, of Hernando De Soto, of Pedro Menéndez de Avilés who built a capitol here, (though Rockefeller chose to rescue the little English-looking one in Williamsburg, rather than the far more ancient but alas, Spanish-sounding one in St. Augustine). Few have read of William Bartram observing sacred Indian rites on a marsh that would come to be known as Payne's Prairie. Today's media-taught

Floridians have learned no more lore than we did, brought up as we were on textbooks and radio. They are most likely to associate Florida not with the myth of the fabulous Fountain of Youth, but with Mickey and his Magic Kingdom—two myths located less than one hundred miles apart in the Florida of contradictions.

Curiously, not much local lore seems ever to have been important enough to be carefully taught. I was in high school in Sumter County when Marjorie Kinnan Rawlings won a Pulitzer Prize for a story about Marion County, just next door to us. We spent that entire year in English studying *Julius Caesar* and the essays of Michel de Montaigne. Marjorie Kinnan Rawlings' name never came up. She wasn't in the textbook. We studied Bunker Hill, but none of us knew Cowpens, or King's Mountain, both crucial, pivotal battles that took place not far away, in South Carolina. We all studied Gettysburg, but never heard of Olustee, or Natural Bridge, battles crucial to the Civil War as it unfolded in Florida. I was forty years old before I read somewhere—while preparing to teach a class, probably—that Tallahassee, where I lived and worked for ten years, and earned my undergraduate and graduate degrees, was the only Southern capital to remain uncaptured throughout the Civil War. Was it maybe just not important enough to my Florida teachers? Who taught them, that they knew Bunker Hill but not Cowpens? I want now to ask, sixty-five years after graduation, wasn't there a manual for Florida teachers, for teachers of Florida history and literature? Wouldn't it have mentioned virtually everything noteworthy about Florida? Actually, I think I've figured out the answer. Is it possible that I studied Bunker Hill instead of Olustee because the publishers of all the textbooks available then were in New York or Boston or Philadelphia, and because they hired editors who were teaching at universities in those cities and places like them, similarly "up there in the North," that all those editors had indeed themselves been educated at those same universities "up there"? Was my education based on a prejudice in geography? Is it prejudicial to grow up and go to school in the South, taught lessons and texts formulated elsewhere? Can the South finally be trusted to write its own textbooks?

I'm not always sure that it was bad that Florida did not show up very significantly in my history and literature books. I've since then winced more than a few times upon discovering Florida in print. Even in writers from the South, the picture is far from universally flattering. Flannery O'Connor's Mr. Jerger tells Ruby Hill in "A Stroke of Good Fortune" that "Florida is not a noble state...but it is an important one." I thought of it that way, too, growing up. I remember snow-covered conifer branches on the Christmas cards my Sumter County grandmothers sent me, and I'm sure I wondered if there wasn't something a little more actually official about Christmas where it snowed, where conifers like that grew, where birds like the ones in those picture post-cards sat on branches, though I'd never seen such a bird or tree. I read all those essays by Emerson, the stories of Hawthorne and Irving, knew something of the date of the founding of Harvard before I heard anything about the story of the founding of the University of Florida, fifty miles away, and I must have wondered, all the while, if there wasn't something just simply more important going on in New York, in New England. My history and my geography weren't as important, I was sure. It didn't help me feel more real, either, when I read James Street explain, in *Look Away*, that "Florida always seemed like a sister with a wealthy Yankee Beau." Truth is, it seemed that way to me, too. Sixty years later Nanci Kincaid's *Crossing Blood* keeps me uneasy, wondering if it is all real, explaining that "Florida is based on lying to Yankees." It was almost natural, then, to hear Barry Hannah's Barry Monroe in *Geronimo Rex* quote a professor's snide comment that "Florida was unique in going straight from barbarism to decadence without an intervening period of civilization." I hadn't caught yet the passion for the local, the sense of the minutiae of home that would overwhelm me as it did when I first encountered the Victoria County Histories and learned that it was possible for every single name and date and story of one's own place to be important enough to write big, long books about. For the longest time I was easily insulted for Florida.

Everything looked better after college when I finally learned a different perspective. By then I knew that Florida had had eleven governors when Walter Raleigh's troops arrived in Roanoke in 1584. That Florida had had sixteen governors by the time Jamestown was settled in 1607. St. Augustine had been the capitol city of fifty-one governors and, briefly, of practically the whole eastern seaboard, by the time the rebels met in Philadelphia in 1776; seventy-nine when the South seceded from it all in 1861. And that the list of those governors included such illustrious names as Ponce de León and Hernando De Soto, even the old reprobate Andrew Jackson. Somewhere across Florida, surely, a teacher told that to a class with a certain reverence in her voice, a Miss Dove, a Mr. Chips, a Miss Jean Brodie. But none of my teachers ever looked that way at where, and who we were right then, with all that glorious Florida history at our backs. Luckily, I guess, that also means that they didn't teach us that none of thirty-five men who have served as Florida's governor just during statehood has achieved anything like the fame or illustriousness that Juan Ponce de León did so long ago, at the beginning of the long list.

Growing up in Florida in the forties, I hadn't yet learned on my own, either, to look at things quite that way. I graduated from college at a commencement which featured Florida novelist Vinnie Williams receiving an honorary degree for a novel partially set in Sumter County. By the time of that commencement I had read nearly every work by Chaucer, Shakespeare, Donne, Milton, Wordsworth, Keats, Shelley, and Henry James, among others, and had been examined and found not wanting, if not remarkable, with regard to my understanding of what I had read. But I had never heard of Vinnie Williams until that program of the fifty-sixth commencement at Florida State University was put into my hands as I stood in the line of graduates slowly processing their way to the stage to get degrees—mine in English literature, which would make me baccalaureate in literary matters, but totally unaware of the woman to be honored with a doctorate in humane letters for having celebrated Sumter County in her first novel. I wrote my thesis on seventh-century Anglo-Saxon poetry, contemporaries of Beowulf, and I was proud of that fact. In the Department of English where I had studied, the teacher of the oldest writer was the most honored teacher, the teacher of the next oldest author the next most honored, and so on down through the ages of each professor's private domain, stopping just short of the twentieth century, English Departments of the era being quite sure that nothing written in that century could possibly be worth scholarly pursuit. Naturally, I went with the oldest writers I could find for a thesis that might distinguish me, too. All the evidence pointed to the fact that I was doing the right thing. Modern poetry then was Robert Browning for the British, Emily Dickinson for the Americans. Creative writing didn't exist there yet. Neither did "contemporary," whether local or someone else's.

I'm far enough past that baccalaureate commencement now to look at Sumter County differently, passing the big green sign on the Interstate. I have come home to Sumter County to see my father out of this life. He is dying of cancer. He is the only cancer victim I ever knew whose disease was clearly, shockingly visible. I think of cancer as internal, invisible, as my son's was in his thigh, as my wife's was in her breast. But after my father's face-cancer was surgically removed, the grafted skin did not take, and he has since lost half his face, the old skin rotting away in the very presence of the ever-growing cancer. It is a grisly sight, which my stalwart mother has unflinchingly dressed four times a day for months.

But I enter Sumter County on Friday, May 27, certain that my father will not last the weekend, and he doesn't. He dies in a mercifully semi-comatose morphine sleep on Saturday evening, about twenty-four hours after I arrive.

If it could ever be said that death is sweet, his dying is. He was told in February that another operation was useless, that he couldn't under the best of circumstances live more than six more months. So my father, never a philosophical sort of man, resolutely prepared for his death. He flew immediately to Canada and boarded a train, him a retired Seaboard Airline Railroad switchman with forty-two years' credit, to take his last train ride, all the way across beautiful Canada, his only time ever to leave the United States. Once back home, he continued to do many of the jobs he had always done, giving them up one by one—driving, mowing the lawn, cooking—as he became too uncomfortable in them to complete those tasks satisfactorily. Finally, towards the end, he could do little more than visit with neighbors who came by, talk on the telephone, watch television. Knowing he wouldn't survive the cancer, he opted against any form of medication, taking only the prescribed pain killers. So as the disease advanced, he met it naturally, at home, beyond doctors and hospitals, just as one might have met death long ago, when a sign proclaiming "Entering Sumter County" first went up along the roadside. My father "entered" Sumter County when he was born there on March 19, 1913.

When the end came for him, at eight in the evening on Saturday, May 28, he was in his own bed, in his own room, surrounded by his wife, his sisters, his children, grandchildren and great grandchildren, all his brothers-in-law and their wives. The family had assembled earlier in the day, not necessarily because it was obviously his last day, but because it might well be, and because certainly it was among his last Saturdays, their day off, their last chance probably ever to come pay respects to the comatose but still-living man. Atlanta, four hundred miles away, was the farthest anyone had come. And even at the end, it all seemed natural; he was not hooked up to any tubes, but was dying as naturally as he could. Though he was comatose, he had been so for only three days, not the long, family-devastating period of months that some poor souls take to die. Half an hour before his death came, all thirty of the family who could get there were gathered hand-in-hand around his bed, singing "Shall We Gather At The River," his all-time favorite hymn, thanking God for the end, and for his seventy-seven years, all of them in Sumter County. It was at that moment impossible not to be reminded of Thanksgiving, the most family-centered of the holidays his clan ever celebrated, and the number of them he had spent in the hummock, skinning and frying game shot since dawn that same Thursday. It was impossible at that moment not to be grateful for the live oaks above, mossy, the grey Florida sand beneath, the brilliant Florida sky over all. It almost never rains on Thanksgiving in Sumter County, I remember thinking.

An hour after he had died, the man from the funeral home was there for his body. He was kind, a long-time friend of the family. He sat patiently while we tried to make plans, finally arranging for a Monday morning funeral, at 10 A.M., to try to avoid subjecting family and friends to the cruel heat and humidity of Florida in mid-May.

We came to the funeral home on Monday. Ordinarily, a member of my family would be eulogized in a church. The Baptist church my mother attends is not two blocks from the house they lived in the last forty years of their lives. It's not but three blocks from the funeral home. But Dad was not Southern Baptist, he was Primitive Baptist, and his church was a thirty-minute drive away. The drive itself would have been difficult to arrange, but Primitive versus Southern is an even more important consideration in putting together this funeral. At a difficult time for her, my mother graciously foregoes the comfort of air-conditioning and cushioned pews in the surroundings of her home church, rather than have my father prayed over in a church he did not consider his spiritual home. His home church is Mars Hill Primitive Baptist Church, very small, overwhelmed by the atmosphere next to it of the Dade Battlefield Memorial State Park, dedicated July 4, 1922, eighty-seven years after the battle, always described as an "ambush" by white American historians. I could never go to Mars Hill as a boy, as we did every fourth Sunday of the month all the years of my boyhood, without drifting away to the moment of December 28, 1835. Major Dade and his band of soldiers marching from Tampa, known then as Fort Brooke, to Ocala, known then as Fort King, were attacked by Osceola's warriors, the beginning of the Second Seminole War, which lasted until 1842, when the U.S. just gave up. Because of Mars Hill, the famous Dade Massacre was the first moment in Florida history I ever became aware of, my first realization that history had happened not just in the abstract, not just in the classroom lecture, but to my family. Major Dade's unhappy end was even more deeply real to me than Juan Ponce de León coming ashore on Anastasia Island, 350 years earlier. It seemed always too hallowed a spot in my too easily fired imagination for the simplicity, rusticity, plainness of the Primitive Baptist Church across the street, on fourth Sundays when we didn't go to my mother's "regular" Baptist church in town.

So we gather not at either of the churches of our parents, but at the funeral home for the eulogy, then drive in solemn cortege to Pine Level Cemetery in the extreme north end of Sumter County, actually within sight of the adjoining county, Marion. This highest ridge in the cemetery where he is to be buried is within sight of the huge stone columns on the county line. I shall not soon forget the deputy sheriff of Sumter County, posted to stop oncoming traffic as we turned left from the highway into the cemetery drive, snapping to a crisp salute as my father's hearse-born casket passed him, just ahead of us, following behind in the family limousine. It was the only time in my life I ever saw my father saluted. I never saw his name in the newspaper, not even the little one, there at home in Sumter County. My family has not been a public one. The limousine continued along the cemetery drive, passing the school where my father had gone to elementary grades.

Pine Level Cemetery is the final resting place of five generations of my Florida-born forebears. I had thought for such a long time that it would be my final resting place, too. But twenty years in Atlanta teaching school have taught me otherwise. My brother has settled in Mobile, Alabama, my sister in St. Petersburg, Florida. When she dies, they will cremate her, and scatter her ashes into Old Tampa Bay. My brother will doubtless arise at Judgment Day to discover that his ashes had been scattered in the mouth of the Alabama River, as it forms the estuarine marsh of Mobile Bay. As for myself, my ashes will probably be cast on the Chattahoochee River, a few miles from my house, closer to my campus, cast there in sweet revenge by a son and daughter whose time was donated more than often to a literary quarterly called, conspicuously, *The Chattahoochee Review*.

But my father's bones will be in Pine Level Cemetery, where his fourteen-year-old son lies buried since an automobile accident sixty-five years ago now. Here, he will wait for my mother to join him. He will rest always beneath the mossy oaks and the Florida sky he found necessary to life. He will hear the strange wooden rattle of the sabal palm in the hot Florida wind. Phlox grow in profusion along the roadside leading to Pine Level's entrance. The frame house of his birth is not a mile away. The store where his mother reared eleven children is less than a mile away. My mother's people, four generations, lie buried nearby. It is a peaceful scene. I don't think many people die this way any more. Nor do people live much as he lived. He kept an old photograph of four generations of his family gathered on the upstairs and downstairs porches of the old family farm house in Dawson, Georgia, before the migration to Florida. What he liked to tell us, over and over again, about that picture is that all the people in the picture were living in that house at the time the photograph was made. A sociologist I heard when I was an undergraduate averred that the twentieth century is the great watershed in human history, and that the advent of the single-family dwelling had made it so. I'm glad. I look at that picture and wonder how life would have been different for me living in the house of my grandparents, surrounded by them, by parents, uncles, aunts, cousins, all of them, all the time. When Dad was very young, Florida boasted of fewer than one hundred miles of paved road. No one had electricity or running water. He saw Florida move from the smallest of the Southern states—smaller even than South Carolina, as recently as 1950—to the increasingly crowded home of fifteen million. Yet so many of the events around his death and burial seemed more like that Florida than like the Florida we live in today. Among his two sisters and four brothers and four brothers-in-law and all their spouses, there was only one college degree. It was as though within the family, time was still his time, that nothing had happened, as we stood there at his grave, attending his burial. I felt as though we might all be gathered for a Christmas Eve party, as we have always done, since we were too well dressed for it to be Thanksgiving in the woods, the usual reason we would all be gathered together in Sumter County. But so little seemed to have changed over the years, as we settled into the events of his dying. It felt the same way family gatherings did thirty years ago, parents and uncles and aunts in control, looking around to see what my generation of cousins was up to, which of us had managed to show up. It was not a bad way to die. It is not a way many people any more will die, even in the Florida countryside, but it is not a bad way to exit Sumter County.

Originally published in *Tampa Review*, 10 (Spring 1995), 5-9.

50079910R00117

Made in the USA
Columbia, SC
02 February 2019